DESPERATE
ESCAPE

To dear Bob,

With gratitude and
appreciation for your selfless
service of love during the
"Russian Miracles of Faith" series
in Superior, Wisconsin.

Mikhail Kulakov Jr.

May 19, 2000

To order additional copies of *Desperate Escape,* by Alexander Ponomarov, call 1-800-765-6955.

Visit us at *www.rhpa.org* for more information on Review and Herald products.

ALEXANDER PONOMAROV

Translated by Jacob Volkov and Alex Swiridoff

REVIEW AND HERALD® PUBLISHING ASSOCIATION
HAGERSTOWN, MD 21740

Copyright © 1999 by
Review and Herald® Publishing Association
International copyright secured

The author assumes full responsibility for the accuracy of all
facts and quotations as cited in this book.

This book was
Edited by Gerald Wheeler
Cover design and photo illustration by square1studio
Cover photos by PhotoDisc
Electronic make-up by Shirley M. Bolivar
Typeset: 10/12 Stempel Schneidler

PRINTED IN U.S.A.

03 02 01 00 99   5 4 3 2 1

R&H Cataloging Service
Ponomarov, Alexander, 1952-
        Desperate escape. Translated by Jacob
Volkov and Alex Swiridoff.

        1. Ponomarov, Alexander, 1952-
I. Volkov, Jacob, trans. II. Swiridoff, Alex, trans.
III. Title
                        [B]

ISBN 0-8280-1428-0

CONTENTS

Buried Alive . . . **13**

Nina . . . **27**

In a Land of Strangers . . . **43**

New Family . . . **55**

The Conspiracy . . . **69**

School of Hard Knocks . . . **87**

The Accident . . . **105**

"God Is Not Mocked" . . . **121**

Juvenile Jail . . . **143**

Captive Again . . . **167**

The Second Escape . . . **197**

Epilogue . . . **221**

DEDICATION

DEDICATED TO THE THOUSANDS of kind, honest Christians in the former Soviet Union, whose life was cut short, who had no opportunity to tell their story; to all those who spent many years underground, in concentration camps, and often in solitary confinement, awaiting torture and death just because of their faith in God.

ACKNOWLEDGMENTS

IT WOULD HAVE BEEN IMPOSSIBLE to write this book un-aided, and I thank God for giving me an opportunity in the United States to become acquainted with wonderful people who assisted me. I express my deepest appreciation to my friends and coworkers who have directly contributed to this book: Jacob Volkov, Alex Swiridoff, Nancy Van Pelt, Joe Maniscalco, Lois Raynolds, and my dear wife, Vera.

PREFACE

AT TIMES THE EVENTS depicted in this book seem as though they were only a terrible dream. However, while still in juvenile jail or in that distant Siberian exile, witnessing with my own eyes the savage brutality against innocent Christians, I felt the urge to tell the world about the atrocities going on unknown to other nations. I wanted to raise the heavy iron curtain just a crack and allow at least a tiny bit of truth to escape.

At the time I couldn't even dream of writing a book, though I did make a few notes for myself. Perhaps the incidents described here may appear to have taken place long ago in some distant past. But in reality the story I present here took place just a few years ago. There are no ficticious people in this book, neither are these imaginary events. I have given the people and places their real names, with the exception of a few whose names I didn't know. Everything happened as written.

CHAPTER 1

BURIED ALIVE

THE MORNING SUN CLIMBED above the horizon, flooding the whole countryside with its bright rays. The sky was clear and transparent, promising another hot summer day. As usual on such mornings, the birds twittered busily and the grasshoppers chirped as incessantly as ever. In the village the roosters conducted their periodic roll calls, setting the usual rhythm to the new day. It seemed as though nothing and no one could upset such a pastoral scene.

Suddenly, somewhere in the distance came the thunder of horses' hooves. It grew louder and louder until it drowned out every other sound. From behind the village appeared a line of armed horsemen, followed by yet another and another. A large detachment of armed Cossacks approached the village. Such Cossacks were bands of skilled rural horsemen who, having formed armed mercenary camps, recognized no authority but their own and often fought each other as each faction attempted to establish control over the countryside.

Bursting into the village, the raiders galloped through the streets waving their sabers and shouting "There's a new power now! Everyone must immediately assemble outside the village near the ravine!" The men threatened death to anyone who dared to disobey their command. The Cossacks drove the frightened people out of their homes toward the ravine. Men, women, old people, and children ran toward it, still puzzled as to what the invaders wanted. The whole village gathered in a meadow near the cemetery.

In the middle of the meadow a deep pit had been dug. The people assembled on one side of the pit. No one dared to ask any questions. They were afraid that any careless word might be their last. Each person somehow sensed that something horrifying was about to happen, but what no one knew.

On the other side of the pit someone had spread a large ornate rug. In the center of it stood an enormous armchair on which sat the Ataman himself, the Cossack's chieftain, surrounded by his deputies. Behind them dismounted a newly arrived band of Cossacks. The villagers stood silently staring into the pit, each contemplating his fate.

Many of the Cossacks laughed and joked with each other. Obviously the armed men were in an elated mood. Finally, when most of the villagers had been herded together, the meeting began as one of the ataman's deputies stepped forward. He was tall, red-cheeked, and sported a bushy mustache, and a bright-red shirt, tied at the waist, which he wore over his blue satin trousers. With an unusually loud, coarse voice, he announced, "From this day forward this area will be ruled by our Ataman." The men behind the chieftain waved their sabers and long rifles and shouted something incoherent. After everyone quieted down, the speaker continued, "And now you will hear from the Ataman himself. Listen carefully, for his word is law."

The chieftain rose ceremoniously from his enormous chair and stepped forward. He was a Cossack of somewhat advanced age and average height. His cunning eyes pierced through the crowd. Stroking his mustache with his left hand while adjusting his fur hat with the right, he tossed his head to the side and began to speak in a low, measured voice. "I will give you land, seed, and all that you need for your livelihood. But for those who refuse to obey the new order there is only one end . . ."

After pointing to the gaping hole in front of them, he turned

14

around and lowered himself into his garish chair. Again his first deputy stepped forward and, scanning the frightened peasants, asked, "Do you understand? Any questions?"

The stunned crowd, paralyzed with fear, dared not move. After a dramatic pause, the deputy faced the detachment and ordered, "Now bring the traitors! Let everyone witness their disgraceful death. . . ." Immediately several Cossacks jumped up and dashed toward the cemetery.

On one side of the meadow stretched a deep ravine. Beyond it one could see some of the graves of the village cemetery. Soon the Cossacks returned, bringing with them a number of shackled peasants who had been hidden in the ravine. As the prisoners neared the assembly, many of the villagers gasped, having recognized members of their own family. Women began to wail when they saw their husbands among the accused. Children, having recognized their fathers, joined in the lament. The Cossacks standing closest to their chieftain bellowed, "Silence! Silence!" Some suddenly brandished their sabers. The air crackled with several rifle shots. The wailing subsided somewhat.

On the very edge of the deep pit, facing the assembly, the Cossacks lined up the shackled prisoners—men who had dared to question their authority. The prisoners had their hands tied behind them. Some had dried blood on their faces, telltale signs of brutal beatings and torture.

The Ataman again rose from his chair and, stepping forward, shouted, "Now mark well, this is what happens to anyone who defies us." At once the Cossacks attacked the bound men with rifle butts, brutally kicking them and pushing them into the pit. Ear-piercing screams from the bottom of the pit mixed with the shrieks from the crowd. Some fainted and sank to their knees. The Cossacks picked up shovels and positioned themselves around the pit as though they had already rehearsed what they would do next.

Suddenly the Ataman rose again and shouted, "Silence!" All noise immediately stopped. Again he scanned the villagers with his cold-blooded eyes and said, "Now I want to see who's obedient and who's not. My Cossacks, there is no need for you to do this chore. Hand the shovels to anyone you choose."

The crowd shrank back from the pit in disbelief. One man attempted to escape, but the armed Cossacks stopped him. Those with the shovels ran up to the people and rammed them into the villagers' hands. Only now did the stunned villagers realize that they were to bury their friends and loved ones alive.

A pitiful, hunched little old man, fell to his knees. His face was deeply wrinkled, his sparse white hair resembling a light clump of fluff. He begged not to participate—his son was in the pit. At this the old man, along with several others who asked the same thing, were pushed into the pit as well—"to join family."

Some, their arms shaking uncontrollably, mumbled, "Forgive me . . . I can't help it . . . I must or I'll end up in the pit too . . ." An indescribable horror gripped the assembly. Heart-rending groans came from the pit. The wailing resumed. Shovels full of dirt rained upon the heads of the prisoners.

Deciding that the work was moving too slowly, the Ataman commanded, "All right, Cossacks! Show these sloths how to do the job right." His men grabbed the shovels and the dirt clods began to fly, avalanching upon the helpless people trapped below. Women embraced their children and wept in despair.

Before long the pit became a mound. From time to time the earth seemed to move as if it itself were alive, as from beneath came the muffled sounds of human cries. The task completed, the Ataman, without rising from his chair, shouted, "Now all of you go back to your houses, and never forget what you saw today." Indeed, no one could ever forget the horrors of that day. In a daze the people began to leave. Some now collapsed in tears and sobs, but most just walked in stunned silence. Each desired only one thing—to shut out the reality of what they had witnessed.

In the village a new power did indeed rule. The small school building served as headquarters for the detachment of Cossacks. As a symbol of the new order, a strange flag with multicolored ribbons fluttered above its roof.

The Cossacks, needing lodging for the night, entered any house at will and demanded food and liquor. When gorged and intoxicated, they would tell the owner, "Tonight, we'll sleep in your house. You and your family will sleep in the barn." The husband dared not protest, not even when the drunken Cossacks seized his wife, dragged her into another room, and repeatedly raped her. Helplessly he had to listen as her screams drowned the diabolic laughter of the drunken Cossacks.

From a neighbor's house the Cossacks dragged a young half-naked and pregnant woman. Her long light-brown hair was disheveled and stuck out in all directions. Sobbing and weeping, she seemed to be saying something, raising her arms pleadingly in the air. One broad-chested Cossack with a long mustache struck her on the head. The woman collapsed. In a few moments she attempted to raise herself, but the same Cossack kicked her savagely in the stomach. She fell backward, groaning in terrible pain, then lay motionless on the ground.

A few houses down the road other Cossacks stripped a senile, decrepit old man and sat him upon a red-hot stove. Neither his piercing shrieks or the revolting smell of burning flesh halted the torture. Suddenly the fire of burning houses in the distance illuminated the evening sky. Some of the villagers apparently had angered their new masters, so the Cossacks burned their homes to the ground. Darkness soon covered the day's horrors. But the people would never forget. One of those was my own mother.

My mother, Nina Usatyuk, although still just a small girl, had watched with her own eyes people buried alive in a pit and her village pillaged and burned. Such bestial attacks raged across the Ukraine, not far from Kiev, during the 1920s and 1930s. It was an extremely difficult time for the Ukrainians. One regime constantly supplanted the previous one, and each new party enforced its own rules, eliminating those who had supported the previous government.

The various regiments of the Ukrainian Cossacks usually consisted of people who owned weapons and bore grudges against the existing ruling power. A group of friends and relatives, in an attempt to bring order to their existence, would band together and argue over ways to improve their situation. During such heated debates someone with a talent to persuade and incite would eventually surface in the group. The others would place him in charge of the regiment and pronounce him their "leader" or, as he was called in those days, an "ataman."

The ataman had total power and could punish or pardon anyone as his whims dictated. But people trusted him and were ready to fulfill any command, no matter how cruel. Everyone's goal was somehow to improve their deplorable living conditions. The Cossacks themselves were nothing more than ordinary peasants, but life transformed them into violent men. While they served in the Cossack detachments, they for all practical purposes had abandoned their homes and families.

Each band of Cossacks would invite their friends and relatives to join them. When a leader had surrounded himself with a large enough number of loyal henchmen, he would then attempt to seize additional villages and establish his own brand of a "better" rule. Each ataman claimed that his intentions were good, yet many innocent suffered and died.

Lawlessness and tyranny ravaged not only the Ukraine, but to a greater or lesser degree all the provinces of the former Russian Empire. From the very beginning of the twentieth century the Russian Empire had experienced political unrest. Political parties of various ideologies emerged one after another—the Mensheviks, the Bolsheviks, the Opportunists, the Monarchists, and many others. Not all of the ideologies were home-spawned. Some came from outside the country, seeking to exploit the political instability. Anarchy reigned as hordes of "leaders" throughout the entire Empire tried to surround themselves with as many followers as possible. Then they attempted to seize power and control the entire country.

Until recently the tsar had ruled the country by the notion of "divine right." In 1917 a provisional government deposed and replaced him. Lenin and his Bolshevik party, later known as the Communist party, orchestrated the upheaval in the country. They arrested the royal family, along with the leaders of the Provisional Government, exiled them to the Urals and Siberia, and subsequently shot them. The Soviets added insult to injury when they renamed the city of Yekaterinburg to Sverdlovsk in honor of one of the tsar's executioners.

The Socialist Revolution had started in St. Petersburg, the capital of Russia. Soon similar events exploded in Moscow and other large cities. Within a short time the Communists made Moscow their capital. Moscow has a royal residence called the Kremlin surrounded by high granite walls. It has several Orthodox churches, one designated for the coronation of the tsars and another for worship by the royal family and their close supporters. Besides the churches it had beautiful edifices to house various government administrators. The Communists seized the Kremlin as their headquarters and began to issue arbitrary commands and decrees for all the various republics and peoples.

The new government did not achieve total control of the entire country in 1917. It took additional agonizing years of violence and terror before the Communists managed to subjugate the entire former Russian Empire. During the 1930s they continued to secure their foothold in the Ukraine. Once again coercion became the order of the day. Ukrainians experienced torturous years of collectivization when the Communists confiscated their property, cattle, and at times even their homes, and proclaimed them to be communal property—in other words, nobody's property.

Those who through long arduous years of labor had been able to acquire a piece of land, a home, or some farm equipment now lost everything and found themselves on the same level as the slothful who owned nothing. On several occasions the Communists came to my grandfather's house and seized cattle and anything else they could lay their hands on. In addition, severe famine ravaged the Ukraine, claiming hundreds of thousands of lives. But drought or some other natural disaster did not trigger it. The Communist party deliberately created it.

Leaflets, brochures, and other propaganda promised a bright future as soon as all property had been confiscated for communal use. The Communists went from house to house, taking everything they considered useful, leaving behind them families without food or any means to earn a living. Out of necessity people invented many ways to survive. Sometimes, under the darkness of night, they hid grain in secure places. Some buried it in the ground, others secreted it in haystacks in the field. At this point the Communists introduced a new scheme to encourage people to spy on each other and report all "suspicious" activity. They created "The Special Department," later known as "The Committee of Government Security." In the West this organization became known by its Russian initials as the KGB.

The KGB collected the information it received from its agents and informants about anyone considered to be suspicious or dissatisfied with the regime. Neighbor reported on neighbor, worker on coworker. The communist authorities quickly dealt with anyone who came under suspicion. Often such people disappeared mysteriously. Neighbors simply surmised that such an individual had somehow, somewhere, let slip a remark that contradicted Communist philosophy. Such reprisals made indelible impressions on everyone.

Joseph Stalin, head of the Communist Party, cold-bloodedly issued orders to exterminate all "undesirable elements" regardless of their numbers. Millions of people starved to death in Siberian exile as well as all over the Ukraine. According to my mother, every day a designated individual rode through the village on a big cart drawn by two scraggly horses, picking up the corpses of those who had died the day before. Stacked like logs on the cart, the corpses were taken outside of the village and buried in a large pit. Children especially died from starvation. Occasionally they also disappeared without a trace. Rumors circulated that some starving people even resorted to cannibalism.

No one understood why, even after a bountiful harvest, they had to give up every bushel of grain while their children perished from hunger. Everyone knew their harvests rotted in warehouses. Yet under penalty of death such food could not be issued to anyone. Not even the guards could help themselves to it.

A plan from Moscow had deliberately triggered the unprecedented famine in the Ukraine. Its aim was to bleed the population of the Ukraine as well as all other republics, thus subjecting them to total dependence on Moscow. To achieve their cruel plan, the Communist officials confiscated all of the harvest. Then they had all grain and produce destroyed, either by burning or dumping into the rivers or the Black Sea.

To add to the misery and suffering, the Communists declared war on religion. After a systematic destruction of Orthodox cathedrals, synagogues, and temples, as well as the closure of Protestant places of worship, they conducted massive arrests of clergy. The new goal of the Communist regime was to fully eradicate any belief in God. To accomplish their aim they enlisted the collaboration of the schools as well as business, industry, and the mass media. A militant animosity grew toward anyone with any religious inclination.

The government banned religious publications, including the Bible. The communists controlled all printing presses. Even typewriters had to be registered and came under the control of KGB agents. Printing or duplicating of any kind, be it technical or educational—even the instructions on how to assemble children's toys—required a permit from them. KGB agents lurked everywhere.

During 1936-1937 alone the government arrested tens of thousands of clergy of all denominations. It abducted religious leaders from their homes, usually at night, and took them away in barred vehicles designed to restrain dangerous criminals. Few besides family members witnessed the raids and even fewer realized that the individuals were gone. A preacher would never again see his wife or children.

The majority of the clergy went into exile to the extreme north or the far east of Siberia, sentenced to hard labor in mines under extremely hazardous conditions. Besides the nightmarish prison existence where they lived under semi-starvation conditions, they had to perform exhausting labor in freezing weather during the day, yet at night had to sleep in unheated barracks. In addition, the prison commandants possessed complete authority to punish as they saw fit. They placed prisoners into cold solitary confinement, where they received only a small piece of black bread and some water once a day. Obviously many became ill and died prematurely, since medical assistance was practically nonexistent.

The government labeled all church leaders as enemies of the state and eliminated them immediately. It often had pastors as well as church officials shot, since party officials feared their ability to unmask the Communist propaganda machine and expose its true nature. After the death of the religious leaders, the authorities forced the friends and relatives of the executed pastors and church leaders to denounce them and their activities and actions or else face lifelong threats and repression. It was a government policy that continued year after year.

Following the arrests of clergy and the closing of churches, secret laws of discrimination against believers went into effect. Children could not receive good grades or even continue their education if the school officials discovered they belonged to a religious organization. If they did manage to finish general education, all doors to higher learning were closed to them. While a few Christians, through a stroke of luck, did manage to study in institutes of higher learning, the overwhelming majority had to renounce their religious beliefs and lead a secular lifestyle in order to get their education.

The same situation prevailed in the business community. No matter how well qualified a Christian was, he had no chance for promotion or for an administrative position. Often such an employee lost all rights and privileges. A Christian's salary could even be reduced. The general public looked at Christians with disgust and even derision as the Communists instigated a hysterical hatred toward everything religious and sacred. Although it produced a corrupt and degenerate society, the Communists were oblivious to the fact. But in spite of all the injustices and cruelty perpetrated against Christians, some still clung to their faith.

The government directed particular attention toward the younger generations. The Communists formed numerous child and youth organizations to build a totally new and "enlightened" utopian society. Through radio and newspapers and magazines specially printed for children the authorities attempted to explain the wonderful future that awaited the youth of all socialistic countries. Such propaganda followed a basic theme. Following the 1917 revolution the Soviet Union had become socialistic. Under socialism all must work, receive appropriate pay for their labors, and become self-supporting. However, if everyone worked very hard the country could soon surpass the United

States. In the process the Soviet Union could then attain such high productivity and accumulate so much wealth that it would be ready for the transition from socialism to communism.

That meant that everyone could pursue his or her chosen profession or line of work, without pay, simply for the love of it and the good of society. Everyone would work hard, honestly, and conscientiously. Their efforts would produce unlimited goods. The shelves of all stores would be full. The merchandise would go to everyone without charge. To attain such a heaven on earth people were ready to work two shifts a day, often with no days off, for low wages. The average person trusted the Communist philosophy as it forged toward bright future. Such propaganda, even in the midst of starvation, police brutality, and fear, had a powerful impact. It easily enticed the younger generation. The idea of walking into any store of their choice and helping themselves to candy, fancy toys, or beautiful clothing appealed to them. As recently as 1960 the dream included images of free television sets and cars for all.

The government now forbade any religious service designed for children under 18 years of age. A child's presence in church meant possible arrest or deportation to a prison camp for both parents and especially for the clergy. Thus Russia, once a most devout and religious country, turned into a Godless and ruthless society.

The Soviet Union had shut itself off from the outside world. All information about economic matters and cultural development first had to pass the strictest scrutiny of the KGB before it could be reported outside the country. The same censorship applied to news from other countries. The Communist regime attempted to convince everybody that all was well in the Soviet Union as well as in all other socialist countries. It even claimed that conditions in all capitalistic countries, especially America, were extremely bad. When a radio or television broadcast information about any capitalistic country, everyone automatically expected to hear about crime, ongoing strikes, inflation, or racial uprisings requiring police intervention.

Lies and misinformation abounded. It was often directed against religious people who allegedly had ties with the United

States and the CIA. Believing the propaganda, many identified Christianity with everything despicable and repulsive. Countless lives perished during this political repression. Many disappeared without a trace because they refused to go along with the atheistic teachings of Communism. Yet amidst such moral decay God-fearing people somehow became the catalyst that preserved the fiber of society. Unfortunately, such honest and principled people, "the Believers," more than any other segment of society had to endure the greatest suffering.

The events that I wish to relate to you hopefully will raise slightly the iron curtain that separated my country from the rest of the world. It was a curtain that effectively obscured and distorted the truth for more than seven decades. Few have heard or know what really went on in the Soviet Union during those years relative to the Christian community at large and the Seventh-day Adventist Church in particular. I hope that those tragic events of political and religious oppression will fill you with gratitude toward God, who spared you from such ordeals.

CHAPTER 2

NINA

MY MOTHER, NINA, was born in the small Ukrainian village described in chapter 1. The favorite of the family, the only girl among five brothers, she was a slender girl with transparent gray eyes accented by nearly black hair and rosy cheeks.

Her father's name was Moisey, and her mother was called Maria. Moisey was a tall stately man with angular, clearly defined features. His wide black eyebrows, a straight nose, and a forceful mouth gave his face a look of concentrated and stern attentiveness. In his village he enjoyed a reputation as the "jack of all trades." When someone's harrow broke down, they would come to Moisey. If somebody in the village wanted to build a house, Moisey was the man to do the framing. Even when a cow had difficulty calving they called on him for assistance.

If Moisey was the outgoing people person, then his wife Maria was the exact opposite—the shy, stay-at-home type, constantly absorbed in domestic chores. She was a tiny, thin woman with a roundish face and rather large dark-gray eyes. People considered her an affectionate mother and a good-natured wife.

Both Moisey and Maria were deeply religious people and regularly attended the Seventh-day Adventist church each Sabbath.

The house in which they lived, although regarded as one of

the best in the village, was quite small, consisting of two rooms. In the center of the front room, occupying nearly half of the total space, stood a huge brick stove. On it the family prepared their meals, and in cold season that stove supplied the heat for the whole house. The kitchen also had a long table with a bench on each side.

The other room contained homemade wooden beds placed along the walls. In one corner of the room stood an enormous wardrobe closet. On the windows hung the customary cotton curtains with tiny blue flowers printed on them. Next to the wardrobe-closet ticked an old wall clock, complete with pendulum and heavy iron weights on chains.

During that period almost all village houses in the central Ukraine were constructed in the same style, differing from one another only if someone succeeded in building it a bit taller or longer. People considered even that tiny difference as a special accomplishment in life.

During the mid-1920s the Communists had not as yet destroyed all Orthodox churches or closed the Protestant houses of worship. Therefore, Christians still had the opportunity to conduct religious services. Most church services met in ordinary homes, called houses of prayer. Nevertheless, believers found tranquility in them. Nina always enjoyed attending the home church services with her five brothers—Vasiliy, Dimitriy, Nikolay, Ivan, and Aleksey—and her parents. She found the people at church kind and caring. The girl loved to sing and particularly enjoyed hymns that expressed a longing for deliverance from the trouble and misfortune of earthly existence.

Faithful bands of Christians fervently prayed together. Through prayer they found the only possible relief from their harsh existence. Daily both old and young witnessed cruelty, injustice, and terror. They saw the suffering and death of innocent people while the dishonest enjoyed many privileges. As a result, only trust in God and hope from above preserved them.

Suddenly tragedy struck Nina's family. Her mother, Maria, became gravely ill. Before she had been tireless, working day and night, not knowing when to stop. All that changed abruptly. Her weather-beaten face, etched with wrinkles, became gaunt, and her deep-set gray eyes caved in still deeper. Even though she had lost much weight Maria barely ate. She lay with her overworked hands crossed on her chest.

The family nursed her the best they knew how, then summoned a physician from a distant town. After examining her, the doctor called her husband aside. Looking him in the eyes, he whispered, "Friend, your wife has only hours left to live." The words boomed like thunder on a clear day to my grandfather. As predicted, Maria died toward the morning of the following day.

Soon after her death the Communists entered the village of Kosikivka and began enforcing their new system. The villagers succumbed to unspeakable atrocities. The Red Communist regime confiscated all property and food. Then they announced that the farmers were to follow new methods of agriculture. The authorities issued orders when and how to plow fields, what and where to sow crops, and what day to harvest. The people had to follow them exactly.

The Communist Party formed huge administrative departments to supervise absolutely all aspects of life. Only those who joined the Communist party could head the departments. The promise of leadership positions and better living conditions brought a great influx of people into the Party. However, along with all these changes in power came much confusion and mismanagement. No one owned any personal property of any worth, creating an attitude of passive indifference toward "public" property or what might be termed no one's property, including the land itself. It led to the total collapse of the economy, bringing in its wake corruption, unprecedented famine, disease, and death to many. Entire villages perished or were decimated.

Because of the misery and horror Moisey decided not to remarry. Instead, with love and tenderness, he became both a father and a mother to his six children. Being a godly man, he coped with his predicament through prayer and trust in God. Repeatedly he told his children, "Our hope and trust is in God only. If we remain faithful to Him, He will save us." He spent countless difficult days and sleepless nights trying to preserve the lives of his children. Even in the midst of such arduous times, Nina recalled, belief in God always occupied an honorable place in the family. Often they would gather to read Scripture and discuss selected passages.

Moisey took his six children to church faithfully. After church he'd return home with his family and prepare a special meal. As if by some miracle, he would find enough flour to make each child a flat cake into which he put various dried fruits and shredded greens. Having spent a week half-starved, the children ate as if they were sampling something sacred.

Somehow the family managed to survive. Neither famine nor epidemics killed any of them. The experience strengthened the family's trust in God and served as a testimony of God's care for His children. All the neighbors regarded it as a miracle.

In 1941 Germany declared war on Russia, and its troops stormed the Russian borders. The military sent all five of Nina's brothers to the front lines. Before his sons left, Moisey gathered his family for a farewell ceremony. They all were good looking, healthy, energetic boys. But it was impossible to dispel an acute foreboding that perhaps this was the last time the family would be together.

Moisey took his large old Bible, and as was his custom, he opened it and slowly and reverently read promises of God's care and sustenance and protection. Then he prayed. In his prayer he mentioned each son by name, and for each he pled for special protection. After the prayer he embraced each young man. With tears in his eyes, he said, "I believe God will be with you. If we do not see each other again on this earth, we'll surely be together again in heaven."

Tearfully the five brothers told their father and Nina good-bye. A few minutes later they stood in line with many other young men, waiting to board trucks that would transport them to the front lines without even going through basic training. Moisey stood a long time staring after the vanished trucks. Finally Nina took him by the hand and said, "Papa, everyone is gone. We're the only ones left here. I think we should go home too . . ."

Moisey tenderly stroked her head and said, "Yes, it's time, Nina. We must go home."

The house now looked empty and abandoned. Father and daughter sat next to each other, tears rolling down their cheeks. But life had to go on.

With every passing day the German army penetrated deeper and deeper into Ukrainian heartland. The government decided to evacuate the civilian population out of the zone of military activity. First in line were women and children, scheduled for transport far beyond the Ural mountains into safe areas. By then Nina was 21 years of age. She also was to be evacuated thousands of miles from her home. Unfortunately her father, Moisey, had to stay behind along with the rest of the male population, awaiting new orders from Moscow.

Nearly a whole week passed. Then a middle-aged, somewhat balding man wearing his faded blue service cap and equally sun-bleached trousers, approached the house where Nina lived. He was the village mailman. In his hands he self-consciously held an envelope. Seeing the postman, Moisey froze on the spot. He knew instantly what was in the envelope. But then, getting a hold on himself, he asked, "Is this one for me?"

The postman sorrowfully replied. "You're neither the first nor the last one . . ." He handed Moisey the dreaded envelope and headed toward another house, carrying a similar painful message to another family.

For a few moments Moisey could not make himself open the envelope. Eventually he summoned his courage, tore it open, and read: "We regret to inform you that your son Aleksey died in the line of duty." Then followed the date and place of death. Grandfather collapsed in the doorway and, while sitting on the threshold, buried his head in his hands. "My dear son, Aleksey!" he sobbed. "Why weren't you more careful? I warned you and warned you . . ."

After remaining in this position for some time, Moisey crumbled the wet piece of paper as Nina sat beside him and began comforting him the best she knew how, even though her own heart also bled from the loss of her younger brother. Her father now repeated her name again and again. "Nina, my dear, now you are the only one who I can still see and talk with. You are my hope and my comfort until the boys return . . ."

The difficult days of war dragged on. Nina knew that eventually she would be forced to leave Kosikivka for an unknown destination thousands of kilometers away. Every passing day brought closer the eventuality of leaving her father behind. When the orders came it meant all women and children had to depart. A few days later Nina saw her name on the evacuation list.

When she had a chance to be alone, she cried and asked God, "Why does life have to be filled with so much suffering? Why did Mother have to die? Why was Aleksey killed in battle?" These questions and others haunted her. She ceased to smile and became silent and sad.

With a heavy heart Nina began to pack her belongings into a small suitcase. Tears stained each item. Nina loved her father, the family home, her village, and the river that flowed nearby. Now she had to abandon everything that was important to her and flee to some unknown place. What pained her more than anything else was leaving her father behind all alone.

On the day of her departure Nina tried to be calm. She encouraged her father with the thought that soon the war would be over and she, as well as her brothers, would return home. Moisey listened to her numbly, then with a heavy sigh said, "May God make your words come true, my dearest."

During their remaining moments together Moisey read several promises from his Bible, attempting to prepare Nina for her journey into the unknown. In fervent prayer he pleaded with God to send her protection and blessings. After praying for her, he embraced her. Then looking deeply into her eyes, he said, "I am not certain we will ever meet again this side of heaven, but I am confident we shall see each other again where there will be no more death nor parting. Remain true to God, Nina darling, no matter where you are and whatever the circumstances. Now go, and may God be with you!"

The authorities had told all the evacuees to assemble at the village office for an important message. Many were already there.

Tearful families and friends cried openly while bidding their loved ones goodbye. Eventually a large bus arrived and two military officers emerged from it. Both were neatly dressed and buttoned up to the very last button. Even their boots had a spit shine.

The younger of the two, a blond skinny man with a child's face, announced that in a few minutes they would read the names of those scheduled to leave then, and all the others would depart the next day. The other officer was a short, middle-aged individual with eyes black as coal. He sported a narrow mustache, the ends of which were turned up. His large hook nose confirmed his Asian origin. Having stepped outside the bus, he lit up a cigarette and carefully scrutinized the assembled crowd.

Fate granted Nina a few more moments with her father. They had stepped aside and began to talk, because Moisey had much he wanted to say. Suddenly Nina saw the postman walking toward them. At first a terrible premonition struck her. Then she reassured herself that perhaps the postman had come to see a loved one off. But he walked directly toward Nina and her father. Moisey had his back toward the postman and did not see him at first. But as the postman came into view, my grandfather turned pale. Nina put her arms around him and said, "It's not for us, father. Please don't worry."

But as she was still speaking, the postal carrier handed them two casualty notices. Nina snatched them, intending to conceal them from her father and spare him the pain, but it was useless. The terrible reality of war, like molten lava, flowed through the land, scarring and scorching every living thing in its path.

With trembling hands, Nina opened one notice and read: "We regret to inform you that your son Dimitri was killed in the line of duty." She tore open the other letter and read a similar message about the loss of her oldest brother, Vasili, then collapsed. At that moment Moisey summoned his remaining strength and caught her in his arms. Holding her close, he whispered, "Courage, Nina!"

Regaining consciousness, Nina began to cry hysterically. At the same moment the military officer announced, "Get ready to board the bus!" Instantly the crowd rushed toward the bus, but the two men stopped them. "Only some women and children will leave today," one of them stated. "The rest of you will leave tomorrow." However, all the women with small children pushed their way toward the bus door, tearfully begging to be allowed to evacuate that day. They were afraid to wait until the next day since the village had already endured severe bombings that had destroyed many homes. It had suffered far too many civilian casualties. Everyone knew that their only safety was somewhere beyond the Ural Mountains. No one wanted to risk waiting any longer.

The officers in charge remained adamant, explaining they had to follow their strict orders. Only those whose names appeared on that day's rosters could leave. The man with the roster, in a strained voice, ordered everyone to move back from the bus. With great reluctance the women edged away a bit, making a narrow passage to the entrance of the vehicle. The crowd stood almost breathlessly, hoping to hear their names called. All eyes now focused upon the officer with the roster as if he were their redeemer.

Finally he read the names of the lucky ones who could leave that day. The women and children quietly elbowed their way through the crowd and entered the bus. Fewer and fewer seats remained empty. The military officer read each name twice. Suddenly "Usatyuk, Nina!" rang out. Nina felt a chill go through her body. The joy of escaping the hellish place mixed with grief over the loss of her brothers and leaving her father behind.

For the last time, Nina hugged her father. Then picking up her small suitcase she pushed toward the bus. Her father's last words were, "God be with you, Nina. Take care of yourself! I'll be praying for you!"

At the bus entrance Nina paused, and for the last time looked at her village. She could see the roof of her home beyond the other houses. And there stood her father, tears running down his face. Nina wanted to shout something to him, perhaps to wave one last goodbye, but people pushing their way in shoved her further into the bus.

In a few minutes all seats were filled. Mothers with babies in their arms relentlessly pressed forward. With fear in their eyes, they screamed to be allowed on the bus. Some even tried to thrust their children onto the bus. The door finally shut and the vehicle slowly began to move. One very young woman in desperation raised her infant, trying to hand it through the window to anyone who would take it. Someone on the bus reached out the window, grabbed the baby, and pulled it inside. The mother ran after the bus, waving frantically, trying to shout something. Her face no longer expressed fear, but hope that at least her baby would be safe. Little did she know what the future would hold for her child.

Nina sat by the window as the bus lurched forward. Before her passed scenes of tragic partings with loved ones from her village. At times she felt as if she were trapped in a dreadful nightmare. Subconsciously, she hoped that it would soon end and everything would return to normal.

The bus rocked from side to side, leaving behind huge clouds of dust. Past the windows flashed familiar scenes: huge cherry trees on the outskirts of the village where children had once played, and the river, a favorite spot for swimming and fishing. Here Nina had spent her childhood and youth, . . . but now everything appeared so sad and gloomy.

Without realizing it, she began to cry and kept asking herself, "Will I ever see my village again? Will I ever see my father again?"

Suddenly she remembered the death notices. She had forgotten to leave them with her father! Thrusting her hand into her pocket, she pulled out the official documents and slowly reread them. Nothing had changed. The same cold words announced Dimitriv's and Vasili's deaths. It meant that she would never see three of her brothers again; perhaps, never even visit their graves. Apparently her two brothers had served in the same outfit and had participated in the same battle. Both must have been killed on the same day. Nina now felt bad that she had forgotten to leave the death notices with her father.

A heavyset woman sitting beside her in a plush winter coat and a plaid kerchief around her head noticed her apprehension and asked, "My dear child, what seems to be the problem?"

Choking with emotion, Nina explained, "Just minutes before the bus departed my father received notices announcing the deaths of my two brothers, and I forgot to give them to my father. I still have them in my pocket. I don't know what to do."

The woman turned, facing Nina squarely. Her large, broad face, with an oversized nose, fleshy cheeks, and many tiny multi-colored veins, relaxed into an expression of special kindness. She placed her hand on Nina's shoulder and in a motherly manner told her, "These death notices won't help your father. In fact, he's better off without them. No, these papers won't help him. In the meanwhile, you must save your strength. Hard to tell what's ahead for us . . ."

Sliding closer to Nina, she spoke softly, "I hear the railroad station we are headed for was bombed yesterday. We don't know where we're going or what will happen to us or even if we will be alive in the morning. Perhaps we too . . ." The woman's voice trailed off. She took a deep breath and with her hands gestured total despair.

A few moments later Nina's new friend once again turned toward her. "Did you say you have already lost two brothers in the war?"

Nina involuntarily shook with horror at the question and, bowing her head, corrected, "No, not two, but three of my brothers were killed in battle." A heavy lump in her throat choked off her words and she could say no more.

The heavyset woman, while looking out her window, began telling her own story. She had lived in a village some 50 kilometers away. Practically every home in the village had burned to the ground during the last bombing, including her own home. Her husband had died during the famine. She had had four children, but three had died from the epidemic of cholera. One son had survived, but the army sent him to the front. She had no idea where he was now, or how he fared. Now that her village was almost totally destroyed, with the survivors seeking safety elsewhere, she had lost all hope of ever hearing news from or about her son. Now she too was leaving, and to where, she knew not.

She paused for a few seconds, then, leaning toward Nina,

whispered softly, "I'm praying for my son, hoping that God will spare him." With a heavy sigh she added, "Even if he dies, I will accept it as God's will."

After hearing the elderly woman's tragic story, Nina felt compassion for the grieving stranger. Suddenly it dawned on her that she was not alone in her suffering, that around her were many grief-stricken from the horrifying events that had engulfed them all.

Only now did Nina notice the young woman across the isle from her. Her face was ashen-pale and dark circles surrounded her eyes. One of her arms hung lifelessly in a sling, while the other held a small boy—apparently her son—close to her. Occasionally she shuddered, and from her chest came strange sounds.

On the seat in front of Nina sat a skinny old woman holding an infant that cried incessantly. Next to her, two boys whispered to each other. Nina recognized the old woman as someone from her village. Now she recalled that a couple of days before the old woman's daughter had passed away. Apparently the distraught grandmother was seeking refuge away from home to save her three grandchildren.

As she studied the people in the bus, Nina saw both familiar and strange faces. But fear and despair lurked in each face. No one noticed the dust pouring in through the open windows. Few heard the crying children. Everyone sat in fearful anticipation of the unknown that lay ahead.

Buried in her heavy thoughts, Nina had not noticed how quickly time flew by. The bus now approached a small un-bombed railroad station. She wondered if it was an alternate station or if the rumor had been false. The officer in charge ordered the passengers off the bus and told them to wait for further in-structions. Everyone left the bus in silence.

As a few still filed out of the bus, the deafening noise of ap-proaching bombers pierced the air. "Drop to the ground!" one of the guards commanded. All obeyed instantly—old men, women, and children. Seconds later three German planes screamed over-head at an extremely low altitude. The rumble died as quickly as it had come. Total silence followed. The officers granted permission to rise and then gave orders to proceed to the station.

The planes were yet another reminder that death lurked everywhere—that at any moment anything could happen. The new arrivals from Kosikivka, Nina's village, huddled together and clung to each other. Everyone was hungry and thirsty, not to mention other needs, but they focused their attention upon the wooden railroad cars waiting to evacuate them.

The group from Kosikivka sat on the ground. Women fed their children with the limited food they had brought from their homes. What they would eat tomorrow or on following days no one knew. Only now did Nina notice that still more refugees crowded the railroad platform. People milled everywhere. Some were dressed in long coats, some in short coats, others in padded jackets, even though it was still summer and the weather was warm. They only knew they were going toward Siberia. Everyone had taken whatever they could with them to help them survive any eventuality.

Children with little food in their stomachs now fell asleep on the ground with their heads resting on bundles or suitcases. No one smiled, laughed, or joked. Every face registered concern, anxiety, and fear of the unknown.

A small one-story building with peeling paint and sooty windows added gloom to the already tragic scene. Armed guards paced alongside the railroad cars. Some went in and out of the railroad station to engage in private conversation. Orders forbid anyone to leave the area of the railway station. The sanitary conditions were unbearable. One whole day passed.

Evening approached, and Nina sat on her small suitcase. Stars appeared in the sky, followed by a full moon. She found the brightest star and started a private conversation with it. "How wonderful it must be for you up there in the sky. You have no idea how unbearable it is to live on earth. We are far apart. I will never understand your life or become one of you, but neither can you understand my sad situation."

Such thoughts brought little relief to her heavy heart. Suddenly a pleasant sensation of warmth flowed through her entire body as she recalled things her parents taught her about

Jesus, the One who had come to earth from heaven—the very heaven at which she now gazed. He too had suffered much in this life while serving those He had come to save.

A touch on her shoulder interrupted her thoughts. It was the heavyset woman who had sat next to her on the bus. The woman attempted a smile and said, "Nina, dear, would you like some bread and hot water?"

Only now did Nina realize how hungry she really was. She remembered that her father had packed some pancakes in her suitcase. The woman offered her a can of boiled water and added, "Be very careful about drinking water. Drink only boiled water, because there are many contagious diseases everywhere. Hundreds of people are dying."

Nina rose from her suitcase and opened it. From the suitcase rose the pleasant smells of her home. Once again homesickness flooded her. She unwrapped a small bundle of homemade crumpets. They had never looked quite so good and appetizing as now. At first she wanted to eat two of them, but on second thought she took only one and put the rest back in the suitcase.

No sooner did she begin to eat than three emaciated little fellows, dressed in ragged, oversized clothing, approached her. One of them was so thin that he looked like a living skeleton with skin stretched over it. They stretched out their small pitiful hands and begged for some bread. An elderly man with a large belly and a face that looked like a ripe tomato told her, "If you start sharing your food with everybody, you'll soon starve yourself. You'll never satisfy these beggars. Chase them away!"

But Nina felt sorry for the half-starved boys who stared longingly first at her and then at the flat cake. She gave each a small piece of her crumpet. The children took their portions and all said, "God bless you, 'auntie'!"

Of course what remained of her crumpet could not satisfy her hunger. But she said to herself, "Now I had better be patient and eat less if I am to survive this."

It was late in the day and completely dark when the military personnel decided to open the doors of the railroad cars and allow all the evacuees in. Nina climbed in, staying close to those from her own village. It was a large wooden car, previously used to transport cattle. Inside they found some straw. Everyone grabbed handfuls and began spreading it in a corner or some spot that would become their "home" during the long trip. Someone shouted to Nina, "Don't just stand there! Grab what you can, before it's all gone, or you'll be sleeping on the wooden floor."

Taking an armful of straw, Nina settled herself in a corner. She rested her head upon her small suitcase that now became her only and most cherished possession. Thoroughly exhausted by the long trip and events of the day, Nina fell asleep instantly. When she awoke in the morning she could not recall where she was. People were lying on plank beds and sitting on the floor. Where was she? What was she doing in a cattle car?

As she sat up, she slowly recalled the events of the previous day—parting from her father, the long dusty bus ride, the railroad station from which she had departed to her unknown future.

The train rocked slowly but noisily along. At times it stood for hours on the tracks, not going anywhere. During such stops people could leave the cars to get water or just to answer the call of nature. Those who had money purchased bread, potatoes, and whatever food was available.

Before Nina had left home her father had given her almost all the money he had so she was able to buy some food for herself. But she clearly understood the gravity of her situation—that she had to be extremely frugal with her money. She had no one on whom she could depend for assistance.

Nina ate a small piece of bread and two small boiled potatoes for breakfast. During the day she tried to converse with others in order to pass the time and forget the pangs of hunger that relentlessly gnawed her insides. On the third day several in the group got sick, especially the children. Soldiers and railroad personnel took people off the train at just about every stop, since many were gravely ill. Four people died in Nina's car.

After a week the entire train became infected with dysentery. More than half of the passengers became sick for lack of the very basics in sanitary conditions. Inside the cars the air was stifling, permeated with the unpleasant smell of body odor, vomit from the seriously ill, and children's diapers that their mothers could not clean properly. The situation was becoming unbearable. All anxiously waited for the trip to end.

The Ural mountain range was finally behind them, and now they traveled through eastern Siberia. As they stopped in the large Siberian city of Omsk, military personnel boarded the train car. A physician went from car to car examining the sick. Solders removed the weak and the very sick on stretchers.

More days of travel followed. The train finally turned south toward the Kazakh Republic. Four days later the train, with its load of refugees, finally reached its destination, the city of Ust-Kaminogorsk. The trip had taken a total of 15 days. Everyone had lost track of time. No one knew what day or date it was. And no one cared to know.

The people—exhausted, hungry, and barely alive from their long journey—slowly filed out of the cars. Nina held tightly to her cherished suitcase. As if by miracle the heavyset woman appeared beside her. Her face was extremely pale, but she was happy to see Nina. "If you don't mind," the woman said, "let's stay together. Perhaps we can help each other. You may call me Aunt Nadya."

"Thank you, I'd like that," Nina replied. Looking around, they noticed the walls of the station plastered with many posters containing Communist slogans and propaganda: "Long Live the Glorious Communist Party." "The Communist Victory Is Our Goal." It was obvious that the Communists controlled even this far away place.

Military officers thoroughly inspected each arrival's documents. Neatly dressed men, with hands in their pockets, paced along the platform and listened in on the conversations of all newly arrived passengers. After the officers had passed, Nadya whispered to Nina, "I think these men are from the KGB. Be very careful with them, Nina. Any careless word, remark, or a joke about the Communists would cause you much trouble." Nina wanted to ask more, but Nadya put her finger to her lips, signaling her to silence.

CHAPTER 3

In a Land
of Strangers

NINA'S NEW LIFE NOW began in Ust-Kamenogorsk, Kazakh Republic. Ust-Kamenogorsk means "beginning of the rocky mountains." True to its name, the city has mysterious and precipitous cliffs surrounding it.

The Kazakh people, who resemble those of Chinese or Mongolian extraction, largely populated the region. For centuries the Kazakhs had been known for breeding horses and sheep. Before Communists came to power, almost all Kazakhians had followed the Islamic religion. But after the Communists took over, they strictly forbid religious services just as they did in the rest of the country. The authorities razed most of Kazakh's mosques and arrested their clergy, the mullahs.

Alone among virtually godless people with a strange language and customs, Nina tried to find her place in the culture. First of all she had to find work. The very first night after her arrival she spent in a large communal barrack. When she awoke in the morning, she discovered that someone had rifled her suitcase and stolen all the money along with some of her personal possessions. Now she was forced to take any job for survival.

Refugees had come from every part of the country to escape the ravages of war and the advancing German army: from

Byelorussia, the Ukraine, Estonia, and Latvia. The authorities housed them in local homes or in barracks. Five or six people frequently lived in one small room. All understood that war raged in the homelands and that the situation there was even worse. Everyone adapted the best they could, enduring many difficulties.

At first Nina lived in a one-room barrack with five women, two of whom each had a child. The trip had somehow changed those who had come with her from her village. All were filled with fear and suspicion, trusting no one. No one discussed spiritual matters or prayed openly. Even Aunt Nadya, who lived in the same room with Nina, said, "We must forget about God and the church if we want to survive."

Finding employment was no simple matter as thousands of refugees in the same situation also desperately looked for work. Eventually, however, Nina found a job in a kindergarten as a housekeeper. The pay was meager, but at least it provided her meals while she was at work.

In those days the weekend consisted of only one day— Sunday. Repressing the conflict with her conscience, Nina felt compelled to work on her Sabbath. She had no one to confide in or turn to for advice on what one might do in such a situation. Sometimes she tried to convince herself that it was only a temporary predicament, that she, in the near future, would find a Sabbath-observing church, and would once again be able to live her Christian life. However, days passed one after another, then years, and somehow she distanced herself further and further from her relationship with God and His people.

After a while she received a transfer to the kitchen. The head cook, a kind, heavy old man, soon noticed Nina's skills and abilities. At first Nina assisted the head cook, then eventually became a cook herself.

Time continued to flash by. Because they were hungry and had no place to live or way to support themselves, many people became cruel. All around town frightful incidents took place. At night gangs of robbers broke into houses, taking money, clothes, and sometimes even people's lives. However, most refugees quickly adapted to their new situation. They learned that life, in many respects, was much easier for those who collaborated with the system, especially with the Communists.

No one discussed politics. Everyone understood it to be a dangerous subject. Sometimes someone in the neighborhood would disappear suddenly without a trace. When the police refused to search for such a person, people assumed it had been the work of the KGB.

Two years in Ust-Kamenogorsk passed quickly for Nina. Gradually she became adjusted to the city, its inhabitants, and to the people with whom she worked and associated. Letters seldom arrived from home. Those that did come brought sad news. Her father wrote only three or four times—that was all. No matter how many times she wrote him, she received no response.

One day she received a letter from her Aunt Maria. It brought tragic news. Nina's father had died six months before. Left alone, he was often ill and had lost most of his hearing. One day, as he walked to a neighboring town for mail, a car struck him. A few days after the accident, not having received any medical attention, he had passed away.

The news shocked Nina. Again questions tormented her. She tried in vain to contact Aunt Maria to find out if there was any word from her brothers, and what had become of her village. When the war was in its third year Nina received a letter from her aunt stating that her brother Nikolai had also been killed. Nina refused to accept that she had only one brother left. Should he be killed, there would be no one left in her immediate family.

More days turned into weeks, weeks into months. Sometimes time passed quickly; other occasions it dragged painfully slow. Finally, the war with Germany ended May 9, 1945, after four bloody years of fighting. In all regions of the country, whether directly affected by war or not, jubilation and excitement erupted. The horrors of war had ended, but a steady flow of missing in action notices continued. In time Nina received the dreaded information that her last brother, Ivan, whom she had hoped was still alive, was also "missing in action." It meant that he had either died in battle and his body had not been found, or that he had been taken prisoner. At any rate, no one knew his whereabouts. Untold thousands of men had disappeared without a trace during the war, leaving their loved ones in a state of anguish, hoping against hope that by some lucky chance one of them might still be alive.

That tiny spark of hope that had lingered in Nina's heart ever since she had learned of her father's death now flickered out. Her heart ached with the painful realization that her last brother was now gone too. The chance of being reunited someday no longer existed. Tears now flowed unrestrained.

With the war over, people now started to rebuild their bombed cities and factories. In spite of all the incredible difficulties facing them, people comforted themselves with the oft repeated phrase "At least there is no more war." However, the people were not free from fear. Quite the contrary, it was now more than ever the norm. No one dared to openly express their opinions and concerns. Much of the information brought back by the returning soldiers and the POW's needed to be suppressed, since it did not square with government propaganda. Consequently, following the war, the KGB intensified its stringent control over the entire nation.

On many occasions Nina cautiously tried to find out if there were any Christian churches in the vicinity. But each time she received the same answer. "There are no churches in the city, except a small Orthodox church somewhere outside the city limits."

Without realizing it herself, Nina was gradually becoming estranged from God and His people. She could not remember the last time she had held a Bible in her hands. Along with everyone else she accepted the dictum that if you talked about your religious beliefs or become interested in spiritual matters, you would create for yourself unnecessary problems with the unseen, but ever-present, KGB. For this reason most behaved as if they had never heard of Christianity.

The intimidated Kazakh population did not dare to restore their mosques. Perhaps in the privacy of their homes or among trusted friends they might perform rituals of worship, but no one had the courage to conduct religious services openly. On the surface it appeared as if knowledge about God had died out among the people and Communism could at last celebrate its victory.

Nina had suffered numerous setbacks in her young life. By now she no longer searched for a church; neither did she have any desire to read a Bible for herself. To state that she had totally lost faith in God wouldn't be true, because she did continue to pray in the morning, evening, and before meals, though secretly. It was typical behavior among most believers as they sought to survive. To have been openly religious would have been much too risky.

About this time Nina received the offer of a private room as long as she continued working at the kindergarten. To move into it also meant that she had to leave her close friend, Aunt Nadya, with whom she had spent almost every day since they had left their home village in the Ukraine. Although she missed her friend, she now had more space in her private life as well. Then a chance encounter suddenly changed her monotonous life of hard work. Into it literally stepped a handsome young man named Ivan who had served in the army but had somehow returned without a scratch.

By that time Nina had fully matured and her figure indeed was quite attractive. She loved to dress nicely, even though there was hardly any opportunity for it. However, she constantly came up with ideas to make something "new" out of worn-out garments. She sowed by hand, skillfully changing the old-looking jacket or the dress into something one of a kind that really looked quite attractive.

In addition, she enjoyed the long walks through the neighborhood park with her next-door girlfriend, Katya, also single. Once the wind blew off the scarf she had loosely draped around her neck. As she attempted to pick it up, a much larger hand beat her to it. Her eyes followed the arm to see to whom it belonged. She found herself facing a tall fellow, blushing somewhat as he extended the retrieved scarf.

Nina turned red and dropped her eyes while she quietly thanked the stranger. He in turn, after a moment of hesitation, suddenly suggested, "Could I not join you ladies?" Nina, completely overwhelmed, could only shrug. Meanwhile the broad-shouldered former soldier just stood there. Then, looking straight into her eyes, he said with a broad smile, "Thank you for accepting! This means I am very fortunate to be spending this evening with a very beautiful girl."

That evening they became acquainted and had a wonderful time just being together. The next day Nina's heart picked up a beat or two each time she remembered that in the evening she would meet him again. Life suddenly took on new meaning. Later came the weekends together that filled not only their hearts with young love, but made the entire world around them seem wonderful and magical. Suddenly, everything looked so different! The romance continued to blossom, and they could not think of anything but each other. Soon they married. My parents were very much in love, and their future seemed bright.

The year 1952 was a truly happy one for both of my parents. By then I had arrived on the scene. My mother gave me the grand name of Alexander, but later they just called me Sasha. Our family life soon settled into a new routine and flowed like a peaceful river. My father, Ivan, was a cheerful, energetic person and no one knew if anything ever bothered him. At times he would get so carried away with his jokes that my mother would say, "You behave like a 15-year-old . . ."

One morning as he kissed her goodbye in the doorway, he told mother a funny story. Then as he gently embraced her, he said, "I've kept the best for last, Nina. Soon we'll have a much better life. I am being transferred to a new job and will be making twice what they are paying me now. I will certainly buy you a beautiful silk dress. We'll get our son nice clothes, lots of toys, and an exquisite baby buggy for our walks in the park."

He wanted to continue telling her his daydreams, but Nina patted him on the shoulder and said, "Just imagine, my dear Ivan, that all of this has already happened, but for now you really ought to hurry to work."

That afternoon Ivan became extremely sick. Suddenly he felt such excruciating stomach pains that he could not even move. By the time they called in the doctor, Ivan was already unconscious. At the local hospital, where the ambulance had taken him, the doctors were equally at a loss. Ivan died within two hours after being admitted. The autopsy revealed that an ulcer on his pancreas had burst, causing his death.

The ensuing events followed in their cold predictable order. An official from the hospital called the unsuspecting Nina at her work place and after a brief hesitation announced, "Your husband has just died in our hospital from a pancreatic ulcer." After another momentary pause the same voice continued, "You may find the body of your husband in the hospital morgue. Goodbye."

"What did you say?" Nina tried to ask again, but all she could hear was the steady hum on the receiver.

For the first few moments Nina could not understand, let alone believe, what she had just heard. She stared at the receiver in her hand, still hearing the echo of the cold words: "Your husband Ivan has just died!" The sentence kept reverberating in her head. "Ivan has died . . . Ivan has died . . . Ivan has died . . ." Suddenly she felt a choking sensation, then everything went dark. Nina lost consciousness and collapsed by the telephone station with the receiver in her hand.

When she regained consciousness, she saw the broadly smiling face of an elderly man in a white coat hovering over her. The doctor cheerfully assured her that nothing serious had happened and, after the shot he had just given her, she would be just fine. In fact, she could live to be 100. Of course the doctor had no clue what had happened, and Nina still could not quite comprehend it either. Why was she lying on a couch? Why did all the people around her keep staring at her? Then suddenly the bolt of reality struck: her husband was dead and once again she was alone.

When the doctor left, Nina's coworkers began to ask, "Who called you? What happened?"

Involuntarily, tears just rolled down her cheeks and in a barely perceptible whisper, she said, "They told me that my Ivan—my husband—is dead."

The women recoiled in horror and almost in unison said, "Oh, no! It can't be, how terrible!"

Only a few people came to Ivan's funeral—some close friends and a couple neighbors. The odor of funeral wreathes and death filled the small room. In the center stood the black coffin. The smell of the fresh industrial grade paint on it permeated the air. Motionless as a statue, Nina sat beside the coffin. Her dark hair, eyes, and brows seemed to blend with the black shawl covering her head. Inconsolable grief, sorrow, and pain were etched into her face and figure. Slightly bent over the coffin, she stared at her husband's lifeless body. She did not cry, but from time to time her body quivered, and then several teardrops would roll down her cheeks and fall directly into the coffin.

Only two of Nina's closest friends accompanied her to the cemetery. The weather was gray and foreboding. Threatening clouds covered the sky, and occasionally a gust of wind would splash cold drizzle into the faces of the three pathetic women gathered at the grave site. Once more they opened the casket, and for the last time Nina looked at Ivan, who only days ago had filled her world with laughter and with so much hope. Fine drops of rain fell on his face. Nina bent over him, kissed the damp forehead, and gently whispered, "Farewell, my love . . ."

At a distance, leaning casually on their shovels, stood two grave-diggers finishing their cigarettes. Now they were ready to do their grim task. They closed the coffin and began to nail it shut. Nina could not bear to watch. She turned aside and sobbed uncontrollably. With each blow of the hammer Nina's body jerked as if the hammer had struck her. Her friends embraced her, shielding her from the sound of cascading dirt clods over the lowered coffin. Soon over the grave appeared a mound and a tiny wooden marker. The grave diggers were long gone. Veiled in a blanket of fog, the three rain-drenched, grief-stricken women slowly made their way home.

The most devastating time came after the funeral, after the cemetery, when Nina's friends went home and she was alone with her grief. Suddenly the thought that life without her partner was senseless and had no meaning began to overwhelm her. The idea of suicide seemed like a way out, and she began to think of the best way to end it all.

One sleepless night followed another. She was exhausted and tired but continued to plod on alone. Then one day she remembered the rat poison they had purchased. Rising from bed, she turned on the light and without hesitation opened the cupboard.

There it was. With trembling hands she quickly opened the bottle and poured it into a glass. In order not to change her mind, she mumbled, "Hurry, hurry, hurry . . ."

As she looked around, the room seemed drab and gloomy as never before. Taking a deep breath, she held the glass in both hands and brought it to her lips, preparing to swallow the poison in a big gulp. Suddenly the baby began to cry loudly. Instinctively Nina dashed toward him, took him into her arms, and began to comfort him. *Now,* she wondered, *how could I have left the baby all alone? Who would take care of my son? I have no one to give him to. What would become of him? No, I cannot leave him behind.*

Again the storm of despair swept over her and she began to talk to herself, clutching her infant to her breast. "That's it, we must both die together, you and me, together we shall die." Wide awake, she lay on her bed. "Maybe we should drown ourselves? No, death would be quicker if we threw ourselves under a train." She had made her mind up. Only when the dawn came did she give in to exhaustion and fall asleep.

The following day at work she avoided speaking with anybody. When someone tried to strike up a conversation, she only waved her arm in despair, and turning aside, began to cry. After work she hurried home to finalize her dreadful plan. She had made a decision. The very next Sunday, on her day off, when no one could interfere, she with her son would go to the railroad station and jump under the approaching train. *Death will certainly come instantly for both of us,* she thought.

Sunday finally arrived—the day that would put an end to her pain and hopelessness. Strangely, Nina almost felt a sense of relief, in contrast to the torment of the night before when she had doubted her plan would work. When she vacillated. Once in a moment of panic and hysteria she had been ready to run to the station that very night.

The day turned out to be as gloomy and gray as that of Ivan's funeral. Mechanically she finished her morning chores, fed the baby, wrapped him in a blanket and, stopping momentarily in the doorway, glanced at the room. It seemed unfamiliar, cold and uninviting. *Perhaps I should write a note?* But she quickly abandoned the thought. *To whom shall I write? Who would really care that perhaps in an hour or two we shall be no more. After all, when people hear of such incidents they only shake their heads, shrug perhaps, then go on about their daily life, not missing a beat. The wheel of time will not stop, it will continue to turn as before and nothing that we do can influence its impartial rotation . . .*

Arriving at the station, Nina began to look for the appropriate place to carry out her plan. People bustled in all directions with their bundles, baggages, and bags. The smell of crude oil, coal, and smoke from the engines filled the air. From time to time a locomotive would release a huge cloud of steam. The ear-piercing sounds of the whistles of maneuvering or departing trains interrupted the drone of voices.

But Nina could neither hear nor see anything. She just stood there talking to herself. "It won't work here at the station. Trains move too slowly here. The engineer could probably stop the train in time. I must go much farther down the track, before the train begins to slow down. The engineer mustn't have time to stop, and even if he tried, it would be too late."

Looking around, as if someone was pursuing her, Nina tightly pressed her son to her breast and proceeded along the railroad tracks. Amazingly, the baby slept peacefully, as if in another world. At that moment Nina neither felt the cold nor the baby's weight nor the sharp rocks beneath her feet. She was oblivious to everything. Occasionally her knees buckled under her, refusing to obey, but she continued to walk.

Finally she realized that the station was far behind with its noise and masses of people. When she looked around, no one was in sight. Thoroughly fatigued, she sat right on the rail and waited for the train. Fear paralyzed her whole body. At times she thought she heard the rustle of leaves, or footsteps, or even heavy breathing as though someone was pursuing her. Although she kept turning her head, she saw no one.

By now she was beginning to think the train would not come soon and she would die of a heart attack or choke from lack of air. "I wish the train would hurry," she whispered between parched lips. "Then a quick death would relieve me of all this pain and give me a final rest."

Finally a train appeared in the distance. Nina rose and spas-modically gripped her child, then raised her eyes skyward and mumbled a parting prayer. "Forgive me, Lord. I know it's wrong, but I can't live this way. Oh God, forgive me!"

The ground began to rumble from the fast approaching train. Nina stood and waited until it would be at the right spot for her to throw herself with the baby under the wheels. She could see the monstrous engine clearly now, breathing puffs of black smoke. The ominous rumble of wheels grew louder and louder. A few more moments and it all would be over—her life, her pain. As if in a hypnotic trance, she kept staring at the train and the gap separating her from the tracks.

With trembling hands she opened the blanket to see the face of her son one more time, to whisper her last goodbye. As she looked at him, Sasha had just awakened and broadly smiled at her. She could not take her eyes off him. That inexplicable moth-erly instinct, mingled with excitement and joy, filled her heart. Again she glanced upward and saw a ray of sunshine breaking through the clouds. Everything seamed so bright and colorful.

Only then did she realize that she had never noticed when the train sped by. Nina once more looked at her son, and he again smiled at her as though he knew something she did not. Once more a mother's tender feelings enveloped her and Nina's whole being suddenly awakened from a long numbness. When she looked around, suddenly the world seemed a good place again. It was as though she had just regained her sight. She even noticed rays of sun reflecting in the puddles from last night's rain. Birds bathed in them and sang. Suddenly she found herself in a new and much different world.

Hungry, Sasha began to stir and fuss, wanting attention. The young mother lovingly arranged the blanket, kissed her son, and in her usual soft voice said, "You must be very hungry, poor fel-low. Mommy and Sasha are going home now, and you will get the meal of your life." As they walked back toward the station, Nina heard the whistle of the departing train and the rhythmic sound of wheels reverberating from the tracks.

CHAPTER 4

NEW FAMILY

TWO NEW CHILDREN REGISTERED in the kindergarten where Nina worked. Each day during mealtime when she entered the dining room she noticed that the brother and sister ate poorly and cried a lot. Soon she learned that they had recently lost their mother. Nina wanted to cheer these small children who missed their mother and cried so much. To comfort them she often spoke to them, fed them well, and helped them dress.

In time she became acquainted with their father, a handicapped war veteran who had lost all the fingers on his left hand. She felt sorry both for the father and his children. Soon she realized she felt an attraction as well as sympathy for the man. The lean father with black unruly hair and dark brown eyes soon returned her feelings. A year and a half later Nina married Aleksandr Fedorovich Ponomarov, a factory worker, and agreed to raise his children—Valya, age 5, and Ivan, age 3.

Valya was a cheerful girl, and when she smiled, dimples appeared on both cheeks. Her light-brown hair was usually in braids, adorned with little bows, and her large green eyes added to her charm. Ivan's face was round, his hair straight, his eyes light brown, and he had quite a pugnose. So at one year of age I acquired a stepdad, a stepsister, and a stepbrother. My mother continued to work in the kindergarten and, as she later recalled, they did not attend any church nor did they consider themselves to be Christians.

During my preschool years we lived in a one-room apartment, an area of 19 square meters (about 68 square feet). The room served as bedroom, dining room, kitchen, and family room. It required unusual skill to arrange such a small space to serve five people comfortably while at the same time being attractive and offering a measure of privacy.

I can still remember the apartment vividly. At the entrance, on the left, stood a stove on which mother cooked meals and which also provided heat during the bitter cold Kazakh seasons. Behind the stove was situated a small closet, in which each family member had a separate clothes hanger. A shelf stored school books and notebooks. Directly behind the closet was a bed that my brother and I shared while we were still small. The stove, closet, and bed occupied the entire length of the room. In the space between our bed and the next wall a narrow bed was squeezed sideways for Valya. Our beds formed a circle of sorts.

Next came a study desk, and behind it my parent's bed. By the window on the right wall was the dining table. The table resembled a large locker. The family stored plates, glasses, cutlery, and other utensils in it. Behind the table was a large wooden chest to store our linens and clothes.

The last wall contained a wooden partition hiding a gallon-sized water container that worked similar to a soap dispenser in American public restrooms. Under the washstand sat a bucket that caught the water from the stand. Next to the "washroom" some nails in the wall provided places for towels. At the door to the washroom hung a printed-cotton curtain.

A home-made carpet, with some cheap nature pictures hung on it, covered the wall behind our bed. In the center of the front wall reposed a large clock. Family photographs decorated the wall above my parent's bed, and homemade mats covered the floor.

The beds were always neatly made. The apartment though small, appeared pleasant and cozy because we never left clothing and clutter lying around. Because we had no inside plumbing, we had to hand carry water from the street. Even though there were many other inconveniences, we still loved our one-room home.

The apartment building where we lived was a long one-story building resembling a barrack. One long corridor went down the middle of the building. Doors to all 20 apartments opened on to it. Each apartment was alike, with families crammed in them like herrings. The toilets were all-weather outhouses located outside the building. No one thought of, knew how to, nor cared to improve the unsanitary conditions for the most basic human needs. One toilet was designated for men, the other for women. People valued that provision, and no one complained.

A dump was located next to the outhouses. The tenants disposed of trash and garbage in it. Once every week or two a truck removed the garbage. Few if any can really grasp the conditions of such an existence. Beyond the garbage dump the apartment had storage sheds for the residents. Our family had a shed there too.

Next to our barrack stood several beautiful two- and three-story buildings. They had apartments consisting of several rooms per family. These apartments had modern, heated bathrooms with indoor plumbing (the kind that did not smell), hot and cold running water, a bath and shower—all for just one family! Central heating systems warmed the apartments, and no one had to worry about heating their own apartments as we did, nor bringing in the water in buckets from an outside source. The tenants of the other apartments obviously belonged to a privileged class.

Valya, John, and I became used to one another. Both my mother and my stepfather did their best to make us all feel we belonged to one family. My stepfather adopted me and I called him papa. At times he was not very talkative and not at all friendly, while at other times he could be quite gabby and cheerful.

I remember how at times, when he was telling my brother and sister something interesting, he would abruptly stop when I entered the room and go somewhere else. For the longest time I could not understand the reason for his coolness toward me. My mother carefully concealed from me the fact that he was not my real father and no one else told me otherwise. Therefore I grew up just like most children, believing that I had a mother and a father. It seems to me that most of our friends and neighbors never had any idea that I was not his real son.

One time a stranger, an elderly woman, visited our family. She introduced herself as Vera and with a warm smile asked Mother if she wanted to read something from the Bible. Opening her eyes with surprise, Mother asked, "Read the Bible?" Vera, nodding, reached into her bag and pulled out a large black book and handed it to my mom. It was indeed a real Bible.

Mother opened the Bible and casually read a few passages. She offered the woman a seat and began asking questions: "Is there a church in town I can attend? Can you get me a Bible?" She wanted to find out a number of things before her husband arrived home. The visitor answered all questions calmly and softly. The woman's entire appearance—her smile, her kind blue eyes, everything about her—radiated sincerity and goodness. By a most unusual coincidence the woman was also a member of the Seventh-day Adventist Church, a person of Nina's own faith.

Now that she had the address of a church and the time of worship, Nina burned with desire to fellowship with believers as soon as possible. Because the congregation had to conduct its worship services semi-legally, Nina decided to go there secretly, hiding it from even her husband.

Now, after many years away from God, Mother once again stepped over the threshold of a church. As she entered the small hall of the church, she saw a pulpit, seats for the choir, and genial smiles on the faces of the congregation. Her eyes filled with tears. Childhood memories from far away Ukraine flooded her.

After returning home from her first visit to church, Mother could not constrain herself and shared her overflowing joy with her husband. Becoming extremely upset, he cut her off, coldly announcing, "I don't want you to attend this church; I don't need additional problems on my hands." Mother explained that she had been born into a Christian family, and that from her early childhood she had gone to church and enjoyed the fellowship of the believers. Ignoring her pleas, he issued one final command:

"If you want to keep this family intact you will forget your church. I forbid you to go again."

Despite his protests and threats, though, she continued to attend church services regularly and was soon baptized. Because Nina no longer felt she could continue to work on her Sabbath, the management assigned her to a much more demanding and dirty work detail. She had to wash all the dishes by hand and peel no less then 140 pouds of potatoes. In addition, she had to sweep all the premises, as well as the grounds around the two kindergarten buildings. If that wasn't enough, they demanded she pull guard duty at night. And to add insult to injury, they halved her former salary. However, Nina was content since she now had opportunity to attend her church every Sabbath. Sometimes, unknown to Papa, she took us children to the services. There we recited Bible verses and poems that we memorized and sang songs along with other children.

Thus several years went by.

At age 7 it came time for me to go to school. I was taller than some, and, as I remember, a bit stronger than most, especially those shorter. My haircut was short and at the crown of my head a lock of hair stuck out as though cut straight across with a ruler. Sometimes I felt comfortable with my green eyes, even eyebrows, comparatively straight nose, and somewhat plump lips, but more often I considered myself less than handsome—a feeling that at times depressed me.

During my first three grades I was a straight A student. I liked school, studied exceptionally hard, and was considered to be a good pupil. In those days teachers often ridiculed Christians and tried in every possible way to undermine faith in God. As a result I went to church with my mother less and less frequently. Suddenly I found the church boring, the sermons monotonous, and the singing sad and gloomy.

During that time I had a friend named Mishka. Though he was a bit older, he was just a little shorter. Blond with light blue eyes, he had an unusually small nose around which were scattered barely visible freckles. He was a lot of fun, extremely cheerful, and loved, no less than I, to play tricks. Whenever he would become excited, he stuttered, but it was barely noticeable.

His mother was also a Christian, but not his father. So in a way his family, in many respects, resembled ours. Sometimes Mishka and I talked about religious matters and our relationship to God and the church. Such conversations usually ended with the thought that religion was not compatible with our lives. At least not now anyway.

Times were difficult, and children living under such arduous conditions matured faster than do children brought up in easier situations. For that reason, at an early age I began to seriously think about religion. When I was 10, during summer vacation, Mishka and I again began discussing religion, the church, and our mothers, who despite all opposition zealously attended worship services. "Why don't we just slip into church late sometimes, so that our mothers won't know anything about it," Mishka suggested. "We'll listen to the sermon, look the worshipers over, and then tell each other what we think." I liked the idea.

The next Sabbath we arrived at the very beginning of the sermon and sat in the last row in order not to attract anyone's attention. The church was a long way outside the city limits. The believers were poor, and no one owned a car. In order to get to church, the members depended upon public transportation. Some had to transfer several times. The buses on this route did not keep precise schedules. To get there on time many had to allow three hours or more for traveling.

The church was located next to a large prison, which made the place unattractive and even repulsive. From the outside, the building resembled any other poor home in the vicinity. A small hallway at the entrance served as a cloakroom. The door straight ahead led to the room where the owner of the house lived. A door to the left opened into a larger room for worship services. It had been created by converting two rooms into one. The congregation sat on benches or on boards supported by stools.

At one end stood a plywood pulpit. Next to the pulpit were three benches for the choir. On the side walls hung frames with Bible verses decorated with flowers or some ornamental design. The ceiling was low, and toward the end of the service on a hot summer day the air was stifling. (Most people bathed generally once a week, and deodorants were nonexistent.)

I often wondered what attracted people to this humble house of worship. The place was not only unattractive, it wasn't even safe. The house was not registered anywhere as a church. It was simply a building that a kind old man had offered as a temporary site of worship.

When Mishka and I arrived the service had already started. The congregation sang a hymn and knelt for prayer. Not to be conspicuous, we followed suit. After the prayer the choir sang and the Sabbath school began. One of the members stood behind the pulpit and asked questions pertaining to the past week's lesson. Everyone present answered them. I liked this kind of interactive method of learning about the Bible. An inner voice, it seemed, whispered to me, "These are not the ignorant people you thought they were."

Following the Sabbath school lesson and short recess, the sermon began. The preacher was a young German man. His pronunciation was not always accurate, but his charm and his sincerity captivated me. I listened to him with rapt attention, and to my surprise, I liked what I heard.

After the service the congregation greeted each other with handshakes and friendly hugs. They encouraged each other with pleasant and kind words. It made a strong impression on me. That very day I decided to attend the services regularly, since it was summer and I did not have to go to school.

After the service Mishka asked if my outlook on religion, church, and believers had changed. I told him that it had and that I planned to attend during the summer. To my amazement he said he felt the same way. Our mothers were delighted to see us come regularly on our own.

Mishka and I began to go to church on a regular basis. It did not mean that we were "believers" by any stretch of the imagination. As before, we continued with our pranks and jokes, laughing at everything, sometimes inappropriately. During services we whispered, wrote notes to each other, and engaged in typical behavior for boys our age. Sometimes Mother coughed in a peculiar manner to remind me that I was at a worship service and should keep quiet. In spite of all of this, deep down inside I felt a strange attraction to the church, especially to the people.

The church members took an interest in us, and after the services greeted us affectionately and asked if we needed anything. I enjoyed their fellowship, and the Holy Spirit worked through my association with them. Soon I longed to act and look like them!

Mother sang in the choir and served as a deaconess. Mishka's mother also held the same church offices. But all of us continued to keep our church attendance secret, even from the other members of our family.

I can't say that I liked everything about the services. Some things I did not agree with. But I could not deny that some of the sermons and the choir music made an indelible impression on me and I developed a deep personal yearning to read the Bible. As I began to read my mother's Bible, a myriad of questions formed in my mind. Immediately I bombarded my mother with them. Many of them she answered to the best of her ability, but to some questions she suggested, "Sasha, you should not ask such questions because there are no answers to them. You simply must believe." Not wanting to be put off in this manner, I decided to ask the pastor or someone else at church who could give me better answers.

Once an incident brought me face-to-face with questions that previously I had only heard about.

An ordinary worship service was in progress. During the sermon, as the congregation sat in reverent silence, several policemen burst noisily into the church. "Everybody remain in your places!" they ordered. Camera flashes blinded us. The officials photographed the preacher, choir members, and everyone present. Two policemen stood at the door to prevent anyone from escaping. Four policemen marched toward the pulpit, where three well-dressed KGB agents in expensive suits, white shirts, and neckties stood. One ordered the arrest of the pastor. A car waited outside to take him away. Two others started checking everyone's passports (all Soviet citizens had to have passports for identification).

Scared, I felt my heart pounding and my knees shaking. I tried to steady them with my hands so nobody would notice my fear. Although I wanted to escape and run home, I knew that the policemen at the door would never let me pass.

My friend Mishka was sitting with his mother three rows from me, and I could not see his reaction. Every member of the congregation sat with a strange composure. Remaining in their places, they began to sing hymns—songs with a message of deliverance. Sensing my apprehension, my mother put her arm around me. "Don't be afraid, son," she whispered. "No harm will come to us." Her arm around my shoulders soothed me.

Two policemen grabbed Pastor Demko under his arms and escorted him outside. The man showed no trace of fear. In fact, I noted a peaceful smile on his face. As never before I was proud of him. His courage and self-control fascinated me. The authorities arrested five or six others along with the pastor, including the choir director and anyone who appeared suspicious after the police had inspected their documents.

"Silence!" one of the policemen shouted angrily, stopping the singing. One of the three men dressed in suits, who appeared to be in command, stood beside the pulpit and said, "The rest of you must immediately go to your homes and never assemble here. If you are ever found here again, you will be fined. If this manner of punishment does not convince you, we will have to resort to harsher methods." Then he took a handkerchief from his pocket and wiped his sweating forehead.

I expected that most of the people would quickly disperse and go home. But to my surprise all remained in their seats, maintaining total calm. A few years later, as I thought about the incident, I understood that what was happening involved a common psychological pressure tactic. If people had reacted in panic, scurrying all over the place, it would have been easier for the KGB to deal with them. It takes a lot less effort to control a frightened person.

Suddenly an old man, holding a Bible in his hands, stood and announced, "Brothers, sisters, and honored representatives of the government. We began our service with the customary prayer, and I suggest we end it with a prayer. But before the prayer, I want to read to you something from the sacred Scriptures."

The man did not go to the front, but spoke right from where he was. Because of his bushy gray beard he appeared to be the oldest person present. Realizing the seriousness of the situation, he rose to the occasion and did it exceptionally well. Such daring behavior for a young person would have resulted in arrest, dismissal from work, or some other unpredictable consequence. But at his age the old man realized he had little to lose. He conducted himself as if he had the authority to lead the church, even though he was an ordinary member.

The old man read the scriptures in a jubilant voice, choosing comforting words by Jesus about the difficult times when His followers would suffer pain and persecution, and that such times of sorrow would be replaced with eternal joy in heaven. The unexpected turn of events shocked the police and KGB agents and they stood there listening as if in a trance.

After reading from the gospels, the elderly man spoke a few encouraging words and announced the closing hymn before the benediction. The entire congregation burst into exultant singing:

"Oh, no one on this earth is able
To sever us from God above!
Let come cold bonds, let come whatever,
We firmly shall believe and love."

As I listened to the hymn, I too sensed the peace that others seemed to have. My knees stopped shaking. Becoming completely calm, I joined the rest in singing. Only after the final prayer did the congregation begin to leave. Outside, two large police vans indicated that the authorities had come prepared to arrest a large number of people. I felt another surge of fear go through my whole body. Right then Mishka patted me on the shoulder and asked, "Were you scared?" I wanted to appear brave and say something smart, but it did not come out right. Mishka grinned at me and whispered, "I got real scared when I saw the police and thought we'd be sent to jail. And I didn't even know what I'd done wrong."

During the bus ride home I sat next to Mishka. I wanted very much to share with him my impression of the incident and ask about his. Since he was older than I, it was very important for me to know what he thought. I told him my reaction when I saw the policemen with pistols on their belts. My friend said he felt the same way, even though he never admitted to getting weak in the knees.

"Mishka," I asked, "why do you think they hate Christians so much? After all, Christians are kind, honest, hardworking people. Where's the problem?"

Peering thoughtfully through the bus window, he said, "I think, Sasha, it's because Christians are such good people and make the godless look bad. Now that the Communists control everything, they have decided to do away with Christians so no one can possibly appear better than they."

"Then Christians are right?" I asked.

"Perhaps, perhaps," my friend intoned in a sing-song voice. For a while we rode in silence, pondering what we had seen and heard that day.

A number of people who had participated in the worship service were also on the bus. Thoughtfully I observed their faces and listened to their conversations, yet I saw no trace of anxiety or apprehension.

Leaning toward Mishka, I whispered, "Why do these people behave as if nothing happened?"

Also in a whisper he replied, "Because this isn't the first time this has happened to them. They've been through it before."

It was a long time before I could fall asleep that night. The scenes I had witnessed that day kept racing through my mind. I could hear the threats of the KGB agents and see the face of the arrested pastor. *Where are they?* I wondered. *What will become of them? Will they be sent to prison? And what for?*

Suddenly, as I lay upon my bed, the answers to my questions became apparent. People by themselves could not be so evil. Behind the KGB, the police, and the rest of the godless people another ruling power must exist. It became clear to me as never before that the basic conflict is not among people, but between good and evil—God and Satan. Without noticing it myself, I was positioning myself firmly on the side of Christianity. The KGB's cruel treatment of the Christians had decided it for me.

The following day, when no one else was at home, Mother sat down beside me. "How are you feeling, Sasha?" she asked cautiously.

"I had a bad night last night; otherwise, I feel alright," I answered.

She hugged me as only a mother can and said, "My dear son, I want to tell you something very important." As her gray eyes looked deep into mine, I prepared myself for a serious conversation. "You are still a child," she continued, "and the Christian life will be very difficult for you. Everything these days is very complicated, and at any time the unpredictable can happen. I have no idea what may happen at the next worship service. Perhaps you should stay home. The police may come again, and a similar thing may occur, maybe something worse. . . ."

Her eyes glistened with tears, but she gained control of herself and continued in a calm voice. "Sasha, you must think about all this very carefully and decide for yourself. You have now seen for yourself that to be a Christian during this time is difficult and dangerous. If you choose to be a follower of Christ, you will meet many challenges. Perhaps you may even have to suffer for your faith."

My mother could not have imagined at the time that her words would become prophetic.

CHAPTER 5

THE CONSPIRACY

ANOTHER WEEK OF MY SUMMER vacation rapidly flew by. Just as before, I played soccer with my friends. Soccer was such a consuming passion that I would sometimes forget to eat or even go home to help Mother with her daily chores. From time to time, however, I thought about my future. None of my friends were Christians. To make matters worse, I heard them repeat crude jokes about believers or make fun of them. Furthermore, I could not share my feelings with anyone. I tried my hardest to act as though everything was totally normal.

I hadn't seen my friend Mishka for a whole week now, because he had gone to the country with his father. Even those closest to me—Papa or Valya—knew nothing of my inner turmoil. Mother told me that it would be better not to risk telling them.

Life around me went on at its usual pace. But inside of me something went on that I could not understand. At times fear of my uncertain future overpowered me, and I began to vacillate—should I go to the church, or would it be safer to remain at home? At the same time, I felt compelled to take a stand for the cause of Christ. Possibly, it was an expression of childhood idealism. Whatever the feelings, toward the end of the week I decided to go to church.

To my great surprise, the worship service went on without complications. At the pulpit I saw Pastor Demko as usual. The choir sang as before. It seemed as if nothing had happened. However, this time Mishka was not in church. After the service, I asked his mother why he was absent. Sadly, she responded, "It would be better if you'd ask him yourself."

As we were leaving the church, a woman, whom I had seen in the choir, whispered secretively to my mother, "Nina, I need to tell you something . . . in private." On the bus during the ride home Mother and the woman sat together while I had a seat directly behind them. Since they were whispering, I could only make out a few phrases. I overheard Mother say, "I understand . . . I am not afraid . . . I must fellowship with God's people regardless . . . fellowship with God's people." They lowered their voices even more, and I caught nothing else.

As we got off at the end of the bus line, I heard my mother's parting words to the woman, "I'll see you Wednesday, 6:00 p.m. at the mountain." Her comment made me even more curious. What would happen on Wednesday at 6:00 on the mountain?

"Mother, can I come with you Wednesday?" I asked.

She thought a minute before responding, then said, "You could come, but I think it would be awfully boring for you there. It's just another Bible study. Besides, it's very far and we have to walk a long way."

I was aware that on Wednesdays the pastor regularly conducted lessons on Bible doctrines, as I had attended some of the meetings. Some lessons were interesting, but more often than not they were boring, especially when people haggled over the meaning of certain passages. But now, more than ever, I wanted to attend whatever meeting had to be held on a mountain. After incessant begging, Mother finally yielded. "All right, you may come, but on one condition: you must promise to keep it in absolute secrecy." I promised over and over that no one would ever learn of it from me.

The next day I went to see my friend Mishka. His voice had a coldness that was totally unlike him. Trying to talk with him, I showed him my new wooden rifle that could shoot pieces of paper with the aid of a rubber band. Then we went to our favorite hiding spot in the garden behind his house, where we loved to chatter so no one could hear us. We sat on the grass under an apple tree. "Mishka," I asked him directly, "why didn't you come to the service yesterday?"

While still staring at the ground, he unwillingly answered, "I won't go there anymore." An awkward pause followed. His attitude was a complete surprise to me.

"But why?" I asked, breaking the strained silence. Mishka raised his head and looked directly at me. In his eyes I saw hostility. "Why? Why?" he mimicked while making a face. "Because, it's none of your business, that's why," he snapped.

Then he got up and added, "Besides, I don't think our friendship can go on any longer. . . . You're now a believer, but I, as always, want to be free and do as I please. You must constantly live in fear of committing some tiny sin." Then he began to snicker, jabbing me in the ribs with his elbow.

It was painful to hear him. Jumping to my feet, I looked Mishka straight in the eyes and blurted, "I think you are a coward. You're afraid of them, aren't you? I never imagined you like that."

It ended our conversation and our friendship. As I walked home, I kept thinking, *Why did it come to this? Why did I answer rudeness with rudeness? Why am I losing a good friend with whom I had such good times?*

Mishka kept his word. He never again attended church.

On Wednesday evening, Mother and I took our usual bus route to church. In the bus I recognized several people from our church. But they all behaved strangely, ignoring each other. At the time I did not understand the rules Christians had to strictly observe to survive in Soviet society.

When we arrived at our destination, the believers left the bus by twos and threes and went in different directions. Christians must never walk in groups and must go in different directions so as to avoid attracting attention. While there was a lot I did not understand, I tried not to ask unnecessary questions, for I saw Mother behave strangely also.

We walked to the other side of the mountain where there were no houses and began to ascend it. As we climbed higher, I saw huge boulders. Among the boulders was an opening, a cave. As I approached it, I saw some of the people who rode with us on the bus inside the cave. I could not figure out how they had arrived before us. The cave was not large, but it had room for all of us there. In the center of the rocky chamber was a large flat slab that formed a table of sorts. Fifteen or 20 people sat around it as best they could.

Pastor Demko shook my hand with a smile and suggested, "Maybe it would be more interesting for you to go outside and pick a bouquet of flowers for your mother instead of sitting on these hard 'couches'?" I liked his suggestion and his humor and was just about to dash off when he stopped me by putting his hand on my shoulder. "I'd like to ask a favor; if you see someone heading this way, let me know immediately. Would you?" I assured him I would, feeling quite grown-up.

For a while I walked around the outside of the cave, watching intently in all directions. Except for the multicolored wild flowers that covered the mountain like a beautiful carpet, I saw no one. I got great pleasure being in the midst of such natural beauty. After the city noise, to which I had become accustomed, the singing of the birds and the snapping of the grasshoppers now energized me.

Having picked an armful of flowers, I returned to the cave. As I approached the entrance, I heard Pastor Demko's voice. "The time of trouble we just talked about is already here. Now each of us will be tested and reveal who he really is. And we all should be prepared to go to prison, lose work or, perhaps, endure tremendous crises for our faith."

His words disturbed me. I edged closer, sitting on the grass, so no one could see me, and continued listening.

"Dear brothers and sisters, I must forewarn you that there are some informers among the members of our church. I don't know all of them, but I know for sure that Peter Dubovoy is one of them. Unfortunately I cannot, at this time, give you all the details about him, but I beg you, be very careful around him . . ."

I could hardly believe my ears, as I knew the man and liked him. He was a tall, good-looking, middle-aged man. When I was younger and had come to church with Mother, he often treated me to some chocolate candies. Lately, when we talked, he asked about my life, my problems, and my plans for the future. Dubovoy had often preached in the absence of the pastor. The news was indeed shocking.

Everything the pastor now said assumed even greater significance to me. I wanted to know all I could. Concealing myself, I continued listening. The pastor spoke in a calm, even voice. "I am asking all of you to remove all religious material from your homes. Soon the authorities will search the homes of all the church members, and they will confiscate anything Christian they find. To reprint them all again will not be possible.

"In the neighboring city," he continued, "a pastor, his wife, and five other people have been imprisoned. They are all being held in different prison camps. One of the men is in our city jail. We need to find a way to take him some food and warm clothing, because the prisoners who admit to being Christians are being starved and tortured. I know that what I am telling you is frightening, but as Christians, who look forward to eternity with Jesus, we must be ready also to suffer and, if need be, die for His name's sake."

The idea that Christians must be vigilant and faithful to the end riveted itself in my consciousness.

Some of those in the cave stated that, if need be, they were ready to go to prison right then. They discussed the extreme precautions that must be taken during church services. No one must divulge either the names of visitors or the places they came from.

In conclusion, Pastor Demko added, "Friends, there is no cause for fear. If God is for us, who can be against us? Let's support each other with prayer and with material goods in any way we can." They agreed to meet again the following week at the same time and place. Then everyone knelt and prayed intensely. I, too, knelt in my hiding place and prayed fervently, asking God for help and courage.

At our next church service, a gaunt, pale stranger stood behind the pulpit to preach. His appearance testified that he was either recuperating from a serious illness or had suffered greatly.

Speaking in a low, but pleasant voice, he said, "Dear friends, first of all, I want to sing a hymn for you, and then I shall preach." He sang melodiously even without accompaniment. His words challenged us to faithfulness and service:

"If flickers your flame in the fire of trials,
Toilsome and thorny your path has become,
Then lift up your banner like a valiant warrior!
Stand firm for the truth, your salvation is near!

The last two lines of this hymn were repeated. Gradually, the entire congregation joined with him in singing them:

"Then lift up your banner like a valiant warrior!
Stand firm for the truth, your salvation is near!"

Then the guest preached a most fervent, impassioned message. After the service he invited those who wished to hear about his personal experiences to remain for a while longer. His name was Paul, and he told us about the arrests, interrogations, and life in prison that he had recently endured. Amazingly, he had lived to tell the story despite the fact that because of his refusal to work on Sabbath he had spent many a Sabbath in a cold cell without food and water.

The prison officials had attempted many times to make him work on Sabbath. To break him, they would sometimes make him stand in ice-cold water for hours. Yet he remained steadfast. Each time he refused to give in, they increased the length of his stay in the ice water. When he became ill, they would revive and medically treat him only to resume the torture.

Even though what he related was serious, he interjected a bit of humor. I still remember one of his stories. When the interrogator, impressed with Paul's intelligent, accurately worded answers, asked him, "What college did you graduate from?" Paul, reflecting on the question a bit, replied, "Hardwood, comrade . . ."

"Are you trying to be funny?" the official asked. "I am asking a serious question . . ."

"You see, comrade," Paul replied, "I was born in a small village, and there was only one school. It was made entirely of hardwood, and that is the only one I have ever attended. After I completed it, I attempted to enroll in other places of learning, but as soon as they found out that I was a believer, they expelled me. And so comrade, I got stuck with the only education I could get from my village—'Hardwood University.'"

Listening to Paul's tales, I asked myself, "How can I possibly compare the difficulties I have had in school and at home with what this man endured for his faith's sake." Somehow I felt a tinge of envy. At the same time I wanted to be more patient, more faithful for Christ's sake. And for the first time, deep inside me there sparked a desire to be a pastor someday just like Paul.

After hearing his story, a volcano of indignation erupted within me. Why was there so much injustice in our society toward people who practiced Christianity? Why did the authorities put them into prisons and torture them there? I was convinced that such believers had never committed any crime, yet they were vilified by the courts as the basest of criminals.

I had heard many stories from an elderly German woman of incredible atrocities that went on in the churches during Stalin's regime. Bulldozers would raze the church buildings. The government mocked, tortured, and even killed believers, especially the leaders, for their religious convictions.

Yelena Hideschar, a widow, had lived an active Christian life. When I first met her, I really did not like her. She was short and fat and strange looking. Her square, cube-like shape sat on a couple of very short legs. Nor was her face very attractive either. Imagine light brown, almost yellow eyes; very dense black eyebrows meeting at the bridge of her nose; flabby cheeks; and a slick, as though licked into place, outmoded hairdo. Add to it her deep voice, and you got the feeling that all of her somehow did not belong together. Yet her flowing, animated gestures, her behavior, and her soft, sincere smile attracted people to her.

Her husband had been a well-known preacher and church leader. In addition to his other talents, he had composed Christian hymns. Many of his compositions had been sung and loved by the people. In 1937 the Communists arrested him, and he died a cruel death. His widow told us that the last time she had seen him he had been extremely thin and had multiple bruises and scars on his face. They could talk together for only a few minutes through a window. After that, she never saw him again, nor could she find out anything about him.

"Why was he tortured so?" I asked her once. "After all, he was a highly educated, respectable person and could have done a lot of good for society."

Smiling sadly, she said, "We are going through a time in our country when the followers of Christ must prove their faith, sometimes by enduring severe tests."

Doubting my ability to survive such tortures and trials, I now felt scared and really worried about my future. I even thought about asking God to deliver me from such experiences. As if sensing my inner anxiety, Yelena said jokingly, "I see that you seem to be ready to face all the hardships and the unknown all at once."

I had a difficult time looking into her eyes. Turning away, I mumbled softly, "I must admit I'm afraid of being arrested. I'm even afraid of the police. But please don't tell anybody about it. This is my personal secret. You are the only one I've told about it."

"Of course, of course," Yelena assured me, "I promise. No one will ever know about it. But I will pray very hard for you. I believe that you can become a true hero for the Christian faith.

"Try to understand that we Christians have nothing to be afraid of. After all, we are on the right path. And whatever you fear most, that very thing will inevitably come to pass. Try to forget about fear and totally commit yourself to God. After all, there were Christians before us who faced death for their faith at the stake, on the scaffolds, and in arenas where wild beasts tore them apart. If God gave them the strength to face all that, then you and I, Sasha, can endure whatever comes our way."

Her words, like the rays of the spring sun, filled my heart with new hope and inner peace. I felt confident that I, like the others, could be courageous and was ready to meet any problem head on.

Summer vacation ended, and September marked the beginning of a new school year. According to Soviet tradition all schools throughout the entire nation started school on the first of September. This year the first of September fell on a Saturday.

Since there was only one day off in a week, Sunday, I had to make a decision: either to attend church on my Sabbath day, or go to school with the rest of the kids.

The last Friday of the summer had arrived and I had everything prepared to go to school. On Friday evenings we always had prayer services. As usual I went to church with my mother that evening. To this day, I still remember the topic of the sermon: "Now Is the Acceptable Time." With special inspiration the speaker talked about our duty to take advantage of the present time. At the end of the sermon he challenged the listeners not to postpone their decision to dedicate themselves to the Lord's service to some indefinite future. "Our day," he said, "is the present day, because tomorrow is not in our hands."

As we returned home from prayer meeting, I told myself, "If you want to be a real Christian, then you ought to be a full time Christian and not just a summertime Christian, when it is relatively easy to conceal your affiliation." At home I told Mother about my decision: "Tomorrow I shall not go to school, because I intend to be in church."

At first I could read joy on her face. Then suddenly she became quite serious and asked me, "Have you thought about it thoroughly?"

"My decision is firm," I answered.

Mother took a long, deep breath, smiled, and, pressing me tight against her chest, said, "I will pray for you and will support you in any way I can."

Neither my stepfather nor my stepbrother or my stepsister knew about my decision. It seemed to me they were not interested in my private life at all.

At the following Sabbath worship I was the only child there. Many church members looked at me with some degree of bewilderment, because they understood that my presence there might cause problems not only for me, but for the whole congregation as well. After the church service the pastor came up to me. This time I did not notice the usual broad smile on his face. He asked me in a serious tone of voice, "Sasha, did you attend church only for today, or do you intend to come regularly?"

For a few moments I remained in confused silence, then, as if to confirm my own decision, I answered, "I want to be here every Sabbath."

He padded me on the shoulder and said, "Well, we are happy for your brave decision. We hope the Lord will help you in this." I wanted him to speak to me longer, because I greatly needed his support. But he, busy as ever talking to others, walked away, and I did not see him again that day.

It wasn't easy for me to go back to school on Monday. I did not even have my study program, and I could feel my problems begin to pile up for me. My classmates, when they saw me, naturally began to ask me why I had missed school the previous Saturday. I told them I was sick, repeating the same lie to my teacher, Zoya Vasilievna.

The following Monday I came up with another story—that I had to attend my aunt's funeral. Even as I spoke, I clearly understood that I would soon have to explain my cowardly lies not only to my teacher, but to the principal as well. But every time I tried to talk about it to my teacher, fear and shame overcame me. I was totally surrounded by unbelievers, who at every opportunity mocked Christianity and its adherents. Every day our teachers drummed into the heads of their pupils that God did not exist, thus sowing the seeds of hatred and repulsion toward everything religious.

The Adventist believers, adults as well as children, endured much more discrimination and ridicule than the Christians of other denominations. First of all, the Saturday Sabbath was a big problem for the parents at work as well as the children at school. For example, a child of either a Baptist or Orthodox family could remain unnoticed by their teachers for a long time. But children from an Adventist family, after the first absence on a Saturday, immediately attracted attention to themselves. The education authorities severely punished anyone missing school without a reasonable excuse.

Diet was another problem most Adventist children faced. All schools in those days required students to eat in the school cafeteria. At the end of each month parents had to pay for those meals. The school allowed no exceptions, reminding all parents that the Soviet system had only one rule for all children and that it applied to all. The slogan of those days was "You ought to strive to be like everyone else." Obviously many parents liked the program. However, the Adventist children could not eat in those cafeterias, because most of the meals contained pork. Consequently, the Adventist parents and their children stood out like the proverbial sore thumb.

I thought much about how my teachers and my school friends would react if they knew I attended church. To admit openly that one was a Christian was a disgrace, to say the least. In addition to my concern about school attendance, I was also quite preoccupied with someone in a neighboring classroom. It was my very first childhood sweetheart, a girl named Larissa.

Every time I saw her my heart stood still. I loved absolutely everything about her: her large, deep sky-blue eyes, her long eye-lashes, her perfectly straight nose, her lips, and her curly, gold-blond hair. At times I thought how funny and strange it was that I constantly thought about her.

Larissa lived not too far from my house, and I always tried to walk home with her. When I succeeded, it was an exciting mo-ment for me. At times she reciprocated my feelings. Her smiling glances and her friendly tone of voice when she talked with me gave me hope. At other times, I was uncertain how she felt to-ward me, especially when I noticed how other guys from my class approached her, offered candy and jokes, and chatted with her. That's when I did not like hearing her ringing laughter.

Now I feared her reaction should she suddenly find out that I was a Christian. At that time I was not prepared to explain my faith to anyone. My faith in God was my personal inner-most secret.

From time to time I had the feeling that never-ending problems constantly threatened me. Walking to school, I always feared that something bad might happen to me. At home I felt a coolness from my stepfather, stepbrother, and stepsister. And when I thought about church, I felt my whole chest tightening in anticipation of what might happen during the next church service—something very bad.

But despite everything, Sabbath morning mother and I were in church.

At the beginning of the service I noticed Dubovoy, whom I already knew to be a traitor, acting strangely. He kept going in and out of the church every minute or two. The service started just as several previous services had begun—peacefully—and I was sure today's meeting would progress as usual. Pastor Demko stood at the pulpit and began preaching. But not more than 10 minutes had passed when we heard some commotion outside. Someone in the rear of the church gave the pastor a previously agreed-upon signal, and Pastor Demko immediately left the pulpit and sat down.

Instantly a short and plump, gray-haired woman rose from her seat and took the pastor's place behind the pulpit and began to read loudly from the Bible. In a few seconds the door swung wide open, and uniformed policemen barged in along with the same three KGB officers we had seen before. But this time there were more police than before. I could not even count them all. Through the window I saw many more officers outside, quickly surrounding the entire building.

As before, one of the men dressed in an expensive suit with a white shirt and tie walked to the front of the church and rudely ordered, "You, old woman! Be quiet, go back to your seat. Now it's my turn to speak." The woman stopped reading momentarily, but then, facing the government agent directly, said calmly, "Please, sir, allow us to finish our church service, then you can tell us what's on your mind."

I saw that the chekist's (an old name for KGB officers in civilian garb) face was contorted with fury. Shoving his hands into his pockets and squinting with malice, he stared at the woman who, without any indication of fear, stood her ground like a soldier at his post. The angry chekist snapped, "I'm not used to repeating myself. Besides, I have not the time to wait till you reread your dumb Bible and pray to your nonexisting God!"

He nodded to the policemen standing beside him. Two of them grabbed the old woman under her arms and forcibly dragged her away from the pulpit. Many of the church members expressed their indignation at the rude, even cruel, act toward an old woman. Some of them stood up, ready for some decisive action. The room became extremely noisy.

Just then I noticed Dubovoy sitting a row ahead of me and to the right side. Lowering his head, he leaned his elbows on his knees and covered his face with his hands. He appeared embarrassed by what was happening.

The head chekist—a solid, well-fed brute with a wide round face, receding hairline, and tiny black eyes that constantly flickered and moved from side to side—raised his right hand and shouted, "Quiet everybody and calm down!" Suddenly complete silence spread through the room. He unbuttoned his coat, pulled from his pocket some kind of document, waved it, and proceeded. "You are all violators of Soviet law, because you are conducting your services without proper permission from the government. We warned you repeatedly and talked to your pastor on several occasions. For some reason, he's not even preaching today. He acts as if he's no longer the pastor, but we know everything about all of you."

His piercing eyes circled the room, stopping on me. "And what is this boy doing here? Why is he not in school today? Isn't today a regular school day, as it is for all Soviet children?" As he approached me, my knees turned to mush. Looking straight at me, he asked, "What's your name?"

My tongue stuck to the roof of my mouth. Finally I managed to get my name out. Noticing how petrified I was, he turned from me and asked, "Who are his parents?"

Mother rose and calmly said, "I am his mother."

"Why is your son not in school today? What right do you have to take a minor to church?"

She did not answer but only sat down.

The enraged chekist would not calm down. Addressing her, he threatened, "Don't you realize that we will prosecute you for crippling the child by stuffing his head with religious ideas?"

His words slashed across my heart. Then I remembered Yelena Heideschar's observation that "we are overcome by the things we fear most."

The chekist turned to me again, saying, "Do you realize that because you are here and not in school, we're going to close the church?" Then, turning sharply toward the congregation, he said in an irritated voice, "According to the Soviet code of law, children under 18 years of age are not allowed to attend religious services. In case of violation of this law, such a church must be shut down. You have doubly violated the Soviet law: you conduct services here without our permission, and, on top of that, you bring children here."

Apparently trying to frighten me even more, he demanded, "You understand, don't you, that you have no right to be here at all? Can you promise us now that you will never come here again?"

I do not know where I got the courage, but I felt as if I was on the soccer field and that at any cost I had to score a point or my team would lose. Jumping up from my seat, I announced loudly, "I am not afraid of you and will continue attending this church." Then I sat down, trying to figure out what I had just blurted out. But I felt good inside. I had just conquered one of the greatest fears of my life. I was not the coward that I had felt I was the day before.

The chekist again turned toward the congregation, asking, "What do you think now about all you have heard, church members? Are you willing to make a few changes in order to remain in your church, or shall we shut it down right now and perhaps confiscate this house from the owner too? I suggest that you elect a new pastor for yourselves, because this one is the first violator of Communist law. I suggest you choose a person from among yourselves for a pastor who understands what is at stake, and can ably represent both sides. Only then can you expect to carry on and live in peace."

For a moment complete silence reigned. Then, one after another, church members stood, giving their different opinions. Some said that for the sake of saving the church a compromise was necessary. An elder would be elected as pastor, and children would stay home. When they grew up, they could choose whether or not to attend church. I listened and felt that they were deciding the whole fate of whether or not I would be a Christian. It seemed to me that it was the unfaithful members who urged compromise.

Others daringly declared, "We'd rather listen to God than you. Electing a pastor is the internal function of the church. Appointing another pastor is not the role of the KGB. We want to be with our children, both at home and in church. If you wish to complicate our lives, we're ready to suffer for Christ."

For a time the police officers and the chekists listened patiently. Finally, the head chekist raised both hands and stopped the debate. "Enough talking!" he snapped. "There are two opinions here, and I want to know which side has more voices. All those voting for the elder, changing the order of your services, not allowing children to attend church, and meeting in this building only after receiving permission from us, raise your right hand."

I glanced quickly over the congregation, noting those who raised their hands. People were revealing their true identity as to whether they were genuine Christians or not. While not many raised their hands, some did. After some hesitation the chekist continued, "Those who are against this decision, raise your right hand." Immediately, the congregation came to life. The overwhelming majority now raised their hands. My mother joined them.

Instantly, the chekist's eyes flashed with hatred. The officials whispered to the police officers, and they spread themselves among the congregation. Something was about to happen. But what?

The chekist smiled with self-satisfaction. "I see you don't want to live in peace. So then, if the majority does not want to submit themselves to our Communist laws, we have no other choice but to shut your church right now. That means everybody must leave this building immediately. In case you refuse, the police have orders to escort you out. And if you resist, you'll be carried out. I will wait 20 minutes."

Then he left. Complete silence filled the room. Everyone had to make a decision. All of us realized that the church would be closed, and to remain inside was pointless. Slowly, people began to stand and walk out. Many had tears in their eyes, as if they were parting with something precious. "Lord, help us," some said, with heavy sighs.

The police officer in charge of driving the people out decided that they were taking too long. Glancing dramatically at his watch to make his point, he barked to the other police officers, "In four and a half minutes, the building must be empty." The police then dragged those still inside out of the building. Among the remaining were several old people, whom they treated rather roughly.

Outside, some of the many police officers inspected everybody's documents and recorded their addresses. Others waited close to four large police vans. After having their documents checked, several church members were taken to the vehicles. The whole incident looked like the round-up of a large group of criminals. One can imagine the reaction of the neighbors of this "House of Prayer." They must have been scared to death.

All the church members stood resolutely by their church, waiting for the final outcome. When the last person had been "escorted" out, the chekist in charge dramatically shut the door. He had a huge padlock hung on the door with two strips of paper and a seal stretched across it. Then he swung around and bellowed, "Your church is now closed and sealed shut. If anybody removes the seal and opens the door, he might as well open for himself the door to prison. Should you come to your senses and decide to be law abiding citizens, then we'll open your church. Perhaps you have already changed your minds . . ." He was about to say something else, but someone in the crowd began singing:

"There's a land that is fairer than day,
And by faith we can see it afar;
For the Father waits over the way,
To prepare us a dwelling place there."

Quickly, more and more voices joined in. Even the arrested people in the vehicles participated in the song of triumph. And now, right outside the church, an impromptu choir sang the words of an old hymn:

"In the sweet by and by,
We shall meet on that beautiful shore."

Tears of unexplainable joy came to my eyes. I too joined in the singing. At that moment I had a strange desire to be among the ones looking from behind the bars of the police van.

The chekist waved his hand, signaling the vehicles to move on. The singing of the arrested gradually faded in the distance. Then the chekist ordered, "Everybody, go home or we'll arrest you too. We have plenty of space in jail for all of you." Gradually people began to disperse.

At a bus stop Yelena Heideschar gave me a friendly smile, and as if nothing unusual had happened, said to me. "Well, well, the youthful warrior of Christ got another baptism in the fire. I see you've been quite brave today and ready to face any problem. I am coming to the end of my Christian journey, but you are only starting out. Some day inevitably you will meet up with even bigger problems . . ."

At that moment I felt both happy and sad. Happy because, for the first time I felt a bit more courageous than ever. And sad because of the uncertainty of what the future held in store for me. After all, the church was now closed. The pastor and several church officers had been arrested. And I kept hearing how some members in whispers discussed having to move deep "underground" from then on. What that meant I had no idea. But somehow in my subconsciousness I knew that my own as well as the church's future would be uncertain.

CHAPTER 6

School
of Hard Knocks

AT HOME I COULD NOT say anything to the rest of my family about what had happened in church. Mother was afraid her husband would leave her because of the incident. It wasn't easy for me to keep inside of me everything that I had seen and experienced at our last church service, but I understood that I had to keep silent.

When I arrived at school the following week, my teacher, Zoya Vasilievna, was standing near the front door. As always she was impeccably dressed. She wore a light-pink blouse with a large bow in front and a maroon tight fitting skirt that empha- sized her nice figure. Her fluffy chestnut hair with large curly ringlets, her lips, enhanced with a touch of pink, and her dark hazel eyes made her look rather stylish. When she spotted me, she came over and said, "Sasha, I need to talk to you." Then she looked around as if to make certain that no one could hear her and asked, "Is it true that you have become a believer, and that on Saturdays you attend some strange Christian church?"

I don't know why, but for a moment I was tempted to tell her that none of it was true and that I was just like everybody else. But after a momentary silence, I lifted my lowered head and decisively answered, "Yes, it is true."

She shook her head and replied in a sing-song voice. "How terrible! Such an exemplary boy, an honor student, yet believes in God. And at such a time, when our Soviet cosmonaut has flown into space and did not see any trace of God there. I want you to know, Sasha, this is very unpleasant news to me. Further, I am extremely ashamed that in my own class there is a student claiming to believe in God. I am certain that among the 700 students in our school, you are the only believer here."

She continued to speak in an irritated tone of voice. It seemed as though she was shouting at me. "That's all right, I expect our system will reeducate you and drive this foolishness out of your head. For now go to the principal's office. He is expecting you." Instantly she turned sharply and entered the classroom.

"The principal wants to see me?" I said to myself. And a thought crossed my mind. *The chekist who questioned me at the last church service must have told everything about me to the principal.*

Our principal was named Ivan Ivanovich. I want to stress here that Ivanovich rarely summoned students to his office. Such invitations only went to the worst students or to one of the best, whom he wanted to praise. Of course at this moment I knew I had no chance of receiving praise from the principal, and so a feeling of great apprehension overwhelmed me. My heart picked up a beat or two, and my feet almost refused to obey. As I entered the principal's office, the obnoxious tobacco smell of the smoke-permeated room almost knocked me over. On a large table were scattered stacks of tattered books and all sorts of papers. Dark wallpaper and even darker old furniture added gloom to the depressing atmosphere.

The principal was alone. Rising, he stepped from behind his desk and, looking intently at me, asked rather bluntly, "Is it true that you have become a believer?"

My chest and throat constricting, I answered with a prolonged "ye-e-s."

With a smirk Ivan Ivanovich continued to question me. "What do you call this sect you've joined up with?"

"It isn't a sect at all—it's a church. And I am not a sectarian. I am a Christian," I hurried to explain.

Bursting into laughter, he mockingly added, "All right, all right, Christian, sit down and let's have a talk." Then he lit up a cigarette, sat in his old chair, and, peering through his massive spectacles with his tiny restless eyes, continued, "So, you believe in God? And you believe that He lives in heaven? But our Soviet astronaut looked through a most powerful electronic telescope into cosmic space and found absolutely nothing resembling God. And do you know why? That's because there was no God to be found to begin with."

I had already expected to hear him use the argument about our valiant cosmonauts not seeing God. At the time atheists constantly used the already worn-out argument. Resuming the diatribe he began to recite the various discoveries the Soviet space heroes had made, including the fact that they had failed to find any evidence of God beyond the earth.

After he had discharged a salvo of ridiculous arguments at me, he burst again into self-satisfied laughter. It was quite evident that he admired his "sharp wit." Blowing several rings of smoke toward me, then shaking ashes off his cigarette into the ashtray, he went on. "If you believe in God, you consequently must believe that He can perform miracles? I'll believe in Him too if He could bring these dried-up flowers on my desk back to life."

As he said it he lifted the vase with the dead flowers. After holding them up for a while, he sharply banged them back on the table. "You see, nothing happened to the flowers. This is another proof that there is no God. And I will never believe in Him." He said it as though I was challenging him.

Again he roared with forced hysterical laughter and even clapped his hands. His laughter ended in a spasmodic cough. Apparently the smoke from the cigarette had taken its toll. His wrinkled, yellowish face contorted from the choking cough. He was an ugly sight, but I just watched him, listened, and remained silent.

The principal said some other nonsense. Then he asked me something, but I did not answer, realizing that anything I said would only irritate him further. Finally it became apparent to him that it was useless to continue, so he barked angrily, "Get out of here! Forget about your God, your Sabbath, and this worship stuff, if you expect to live a safe and happy life." Leaving his office, I felt a sense of relief. As if another difficult obstacle or phase of my life was now behind me.

When I returned to class, I felt the intent stares of my classmates. Some of them sniggered and whispered among themselves. Later, during recess, they showered me with a barrage of questions. "Is it true, Sasha, that you are a sectarian?"

"Is it true, that in your sect they sacrifice children? Is it really true that your pastor and your church members are American spies?"

They hurled all sorts of questions at me. Some of them I could answer. But many came from sheer mockery.

At that time the Soviet propaganda spread the most absurd rumors about Christians, such as that almost all believers had been recruited into American espionage rings. Other rumors stated that during church services children were sacrificed, so that every church member present could drink at least one gulp of a child's warm blood. Allegedly the KGB had already apprehended participants in such services and had documented everything. Another accusation stated that during their services church members participated in immoral games in dark rooms behind locked doors. The KGB had invented a lot of other nonsense just to slander and smear those who opposed the general direction of Communism and who suddenly, for some reason, began to believe in God and view the world in which they lived differently.

That day I came home extremely upset. Even mother's solicitous questions, whether everything was all right with me, began to irritate me. More than anything I wanted to run out of the house as soon as possible, and forgetting everything just play soccer with my neighborhood friends. A good game of soccer had always been my favorite pastime, but today I especially felt like kicking something.

The game was already in progress on the soccer field. As usual, I ran to the center of the field to join one of the teams in what seemed to be an exciting game. But just as soon as I appeared on the field, the game suddenly stopped. And again I felt piercing stares from all around and noticed sarcastic smirks on my friends' faces.

For a couple seconds I could not understand what had happened. But when I saw among the players some of the boys from my class, I understood that here too they knew that I was a believer. And it meant that except for contempt and ridicule I could not expect much of anything else.

One of the boys, Vovka, blurted, "Hey, guys, Sasha is a sectarian. I don't think he's allowed to play soccer. He has to pray and read the Bible every day." People in our neighborhood referred to Vovka as "Red." Everyone knew that he was a poor student, and as a soccer player he wasn't much better. Now he had a chance to distinguish himself as an agitator.

"Hey, you, haven't you cracked your skull yet from bowing so low to your God?" I heard another wisecrack from a different direction. The sarcastic words sounded like thunder in my ears. My most favorite area next to my home, where I spent days chasing a soccer ball with these boys, had become hostile to me. Not too long ago many of these same boys had thought themselves to be lucky when they got to play on the same team with me. Now they looked at me as if I were some kind of kook. Also, those who had studied with me and even did homework with me used to treat me with respect because I was the class president. Now my world had turned upside down, and everybody walked away from me.

The reality of it finally hit me like a ton of bricks when the boys went to the other side of the field and resumed their game. I cannot put into words the feeling of abandonment and despair that filled me. At that moment I wished the ground would open up and swallow me.

After realizing that no one wanted to play with me, I ran to a small park not far from our home. Usually I walked through the park with my friends and had a lot of fun there, but now I was all alone. The park had one special bench where we used to sit, tell jokes, laugh, and sing our favorite songs. I came to the bench, sat on it, lowered my head, and just wept. Somehow I could not explain to myself why I felt so hurt. I just wanted to cry, and I did.

An old woman, as she passed by with her little fluffy dog on a leash, stopped and asked, "What happened, sonny?" I didn't feel like talking to anyone. Leaping up as if stung by a bee, I ran blindly off. Finally I stopped and sat on the ground in the shade of a large tree.

One question tormented me: "What do I do now?"

I recalled my meeting with the school principal and the feeling of elation I had had after my talk with him. But now I felt humiliated and rejected by all my friends. I had always enjoyed being a leader. Now I was a nobody.

The strangest thoughts raced through my head. Sometimes I wanted to be the same old Sasha I had been before. Here I remembered the words of Jesus set in a poem that I had recently memorized and recited at one of the church services.

"And those who choose to follow me should
never turn around.
But onward press ahead without a
backward glance.
And for my valiant heroes let the call resound:
'I'll sooner die on battlefield than yield the
hallowed ground.'"

I was beginning to understand that what was happening to me now was the very test of faith I had often heard about in sermons. I recalled Yelena Heideschar's stories about those Christians who suffered incredible tortures and even death for their faith. "But after all, nothing like it had ever happened to me before," I whispered to myself.

Finally I got up, wiped the tears off my face, and resolutely reminded myself that to be a real Christian was to be a real man and I had no business acting like I had. Thrusting my hands into my pockets, I headed for home.

At home family council was in session. As soon as I walked in, the conversation stopped abruptly. I felt they had been talking about me. Breaking the silence, Father suddenly snapped, "You actually decided to go to church with Mother regularly?"

Without any hesitation I answered "Yes." And then added, "Is that bad?"

My stepfather rose from his seat and thrust his face in front of mine. I clearly saw the wrinkles, pores, and stubble on his un-shaven face and felt his breathing. His angry eyes stared directly into mine as he began, "I don't exactly know what they might do to you for going to church on Saturdays, but I am convinced that sooner or later you will run into problems you won't be able to handle. So take my advice, stop toying with this foolishness and start acting like every other normal kid." Then he lapsed into total silence. Only mother's kind eyes silently expressed support and understanding.

For some time he stood beside me, expecting an answer. Although I had much I wanted to say to him just then, I was afraid of his anger. So I kept silent.

My stepbrother and stepsister suddenly came to life and began to talk to me, saying that believers can secretly believe and no one would ever know anything about it, so there won't be any reason for fear. I could hardly hear what they had said, be-cause I was already worrying about tomorrow. After all, I had to go to school, where I could expect new problems.

School had become a place of unending derision and mock-ery. As I would enter my classroom, I would hear, "Hey, guys, the saint has just walked in! Maybe we should ask him to pray for us?" Laughter assaulted me from all directions. It was com-mon for two or three boys to run up to me, snatch my briefcase out of my hands, and scatter the contents with wild guffaws. Sometimes they would shove me from behind so that I would fall in the presence of everybody. Then I would hear someone say, "Where is your God? Why doesn't he help you?" Quite often my teacher witnessed the incidents but pretended not to notice. Strange as it may seem, I began to get used to all of it.

One day after school, when I was getting ready to go home, a classmate named Kolya came up to me and said that he wanted to talk with me. For some reason we wound up going behind the school. Ordinarily no one was ever there after school. But when I saw three other guys staring at us with malicious grins on their faces I became apprehensive. As we approached the group, one of them asked me, "Now tell us 'saint,' will you continue to go to that church of yours or not?" Instantly I knew there would be a fight. I began to explain that it was my personal business and that they didn't need to worry about it.

To be honest, I wasn't afraid of the boys. They were the worst students in my class. I could handle any one of them singly any day, but there were four of them. One of them suddenly shouted, "Beat the saint!"—and at the same moment I felt a powerful blow on the back of my head. All four of the boys jumped on top of me and began to pelt me with their fists. As I fell to the ground I felt something warm spreading over my face.

Covering my face with my hands, I curled into a ball. I felt a forceful kick in the small of my back and then another and another, as they shouted, "This one is for your Jesus, and this one for your Lord! And this one is for your stupid church, the way to which you'll soon forget."

The blows kept coming, accompanied by loud malicious laughter. "Well, where is your God now? Why isn't He helping you now? We can do to you whatever we please, and He won't be able to protect you!"

Everything swam before my eyes as if in a fog. Pain radiated from every part of my body, and my head felt heavy and hot. I even thought I was about to lose consciousness. When I opened my eyes, right in front of me I saw someone's feet in white socks. With difficulty I raised my head and couldn't believe my eyes— in front of me stood Larissa. *I must be hallucinating, my mind is playing tricks on me,* I thought. But no, I distinctly saw Larissa's face. She squatted beside me and looked at me with sympathy. Then she took out a handkerchief and began to wipe my face.

My pain mingled with the joy of her touch. As I tried to get up, I noticed that blood covered my hands. Larissa gave me her hand and helped me to my feet. I was a mess and felt awkward in her presence. She apparently sensed my embarrassment, smiled, and said, "You look like a real knight fresh from combat."

I looked around and could see no one. My four attackers had become scared and fled. But my whole school uniform was dirty, with holes in my pants, and my white shirt had blood all over it. I could not allow myself to appear weak in front of the girl of my dreams, and summoning all my strength, I began to straighten my clothes.

"Here, let me help you," Larissa said. She put one arm around me and with the other she began to wipe my face with a handkerchief. Finding myself in her embrace, I forgot everything that had just happened to me. As Larissa gently wiped the blood from my face, she kept saying, "What did those fools beat you for?" Her classroom was next to mine, so she had not as yet heard that I had attended church and had become a public disgrace. Somehow, I felt it was not the best time for confessions and offered no explanation. Nor did she press the issue.

I wanted to embrace her, but because of my indecision my hands just hung there lifelessly, and I continued to stand there as if rooted to the ground. Finally, she said, "Sasha, how about going back to school, where you can wash and clean-up a bit, then we could walk home together."

"Yes, of course," I quickly answered. Grabbing my briefcase, I headed toward the school. Larissa walked beside me. That had to be the greatest moment of my life!

On the way home, Larissa suddenly took my hand and asked, "Sasha, have you ever really loved anyone?"

Flustered by such an unexpected question, I asked her, "How about you? Have you ever loved anyone for real?"

Laughing, she replied, "I asked you first, and you must answer, and then you can ask me . . ."

I could hardly have imagined a more wonderful question, but why was it so hard for me to answer? Why was I so confused and tongue-tied? It was my first admission of love. "You know what, Larissa?" I said softly. "In the first grade, when I saw you for the first time, I liked you a lot and wanted you to like me too."

"Did you like me or did you love me?" she interrupted.

Blood rushed to my head. "Larissa, I loved you from the moment I saw you and love you now even more."

"I know, I know," she said confidently. "It is called 'Love at first sight,' right?"

She gave another round of ringing laughter that sounded like spilled beads on a marble floor. It felt so wonderfully pleasant and warm. An inexplicable joy and excitement overwhelmed me. As we looked at each other, without realizing it we had stopped walking. Larissa's beautiful eyes and her broad eyelashes were so close to me. Without realizing it, I embraced her and with my swollen lips touched her cheek. It was my very first kiss. We reached her house, and when she disappeared behind the door, it dawned on me that I hadn't asked her if she loved me. I was mad at myself for having missed the golden opportunity.

Suddenly, as though the anesthesia had worn off, the pain returned with a vengeance as I trudged toward home, dragging my feet on the ground. I must have been quite a sight.

A few more days passed, days filled with emotional and mental anguish.

One evening an unexpected guest paid us a visit—my teacher, Zoya Vasilievna. To our total surprise, she was exceedingly gracious and pleasant, as never before. Full of compliments, she told my mother that I was an exemplary student, that a great future awaited me, because I really was a talented and gifted boy, and on and on.

Mother looked at her with surprise in her eyes. After all, ever since it had become known that I attended church, her negative attitude toward me had been quite obvious. Then, unexpectedly, Zoya softly asked, "Nina Alexandrovna, do you possibly own a Bible?" And before she received an answer, she continued, "I really would like to read this book. I have heard so much about the Bible, both good and bad. And now I have a desire to find out for myself . . ."

Astounded by such an unexpected question, Mother reverently brought out the Bible and handed it to the woman. Realizing that I was still sitting next to her and seeing everything, my teacher, with a friendly smile, turned to me and said, "Sasha, perhaps you'd like to go out for a walk while your mother and I have our little chat . . . ?"

Still a bit confused, not fully realizing what was going on, I quickly went outside and headed for the park. But I was also elated. Imagine, my teacher, Zoya Vasilievna, had developed an interest in the Bible. Perhaps soon she would become a believer. I did not want to think about how many times she had ridiculed me in front of the whole class. At the moment I was happy for her and wanted to be of some help to her.

When I returned home, the woman was gone. But Mother's beaming face indicated that the conversation with her guest had indeed been successful.

From the following day onward my school life changed drastically. My teacher had now become my friend. If someone hurled a rude remark toward me, she defended me. Naturally I was happy about such a turn of events.

After a few days Zoya Vasilievna again paid us a visit. And once again they had a long private conversation. As Mother later told me, my presence would have made the woman uncomfortable as she asked questions about the Bible.

Several days later Zoya asked Mother, "Could you possibly take me along to one of your Saturday worship services?" My mother tried to explain to her that none were being held, because the authorities had closed the little church. But my teacher persisted. "Perhaps there are just small groups meeting somewhere? I really would like to join you and be with believing people."

After some hesitation Mother agreed to take her to one of the illegal "underground" worship services. The church members in our town at that time had divided into several small groups and met by rotation in each other's homes. Such meetings usually consisted of some five to seven and occasionally 10 people. They followed strict rules of secrecy. For example, they did not sing lest the neighbors become suspicious. But each service began and ended with a reading from the hymnal. Almost everybody took turns preaching, both men and women. However, every detail was well organized, and the groups maintained careful discipline.

Sometimes the KGB succeeded in tracking down such underground services. On such occasions the police would burst in and reprisals would begin. The authorities would arrest everybody present and hold them for questioning for several days. Whoever hosted the meeting place received heavy additional fines. For this reason the groups quite often met very early in the morning when it was still dark outside. They would then discuss strategies for conducting the clandestine church services.

One such method had all present sitting around a table set for a meal with dishes and food in place. The service would begin, usually by reading hand-copied Bible passages. If someone saw a police officer through the window, the members would immediately start eating. The underground churches had many other ways of disguising the worship services.

And so Mother brought my teacher to one of the Sabbath services. The kind and trusting Christians surrounded the new guest with warm and sincere attention. Zoya, liking everything she had seen and heard, expressed a desire to continue to attend similar services.

Because of her interest, the members let her meet our pastor. At that time only a few church members knew of his whereabouts. The pastor answered a lot of Zoya Vasilievna's different questions. Afterward they accepted her into the group as a trusted member, and she began regularly attending the services, which in our part of town were conducted by a man named Peter, the deacon of our congregation.

Everyone knew the deacon as a kind and soft-hearted person. Once, during a conversation with my mother about the teacher, Peter said, "Now, there is a truly sincere woman. Soon she will become a member of our church and will be a great help to us. After all, we do need well-educated people like her."

"Are you sure, Peter, that this woman comes to church with good intentions?" my mother asked him.

"Nina, you just have to trust people more," he curtly replied. "I am convinced that this woman will indeed become a fine Christian. If not, I could begin to doubt even my own faith. . . ."

Zoya Vasilievna received a Bible and some other printed religious material to read. At that time we treated all printed religious literature as a rare treasure. It had been some 40 years since we had been able to publish such things openly in our country. Searches and subsequent arrests had confiscated most such books and publications. What still remained we treated as sacred relics.

Usually the church members used Christian books copied on the typewriter, or more often by hand. Even the use of a typewriter was dangerous. According to Communist interpretation of the law, only the government had the right to publish, either through its own agencies or by special permit. And if the KGB found a typewriter in someone's possession, that person could be jailed for three to five years, plus have personal property seized.

My teacher once had an opportunity to be present at a special communion service. Her reaction couldn't have been more positive. She even expressed a desire to be baptized in the near future and become a regular church member.

Now I went to school calmly and confidently, knowing that I had a trustworthy person on my side. She would come to my aid, and if need be, defend me. Then everything changed drastically.

To our surprise Zoya Vasilievna suddenly and sharply attacked Adventists on the radio. Later she appeared even on TV. In her speeches she criticized, denounced, and derided the Christian outlook on life and the very services she had attended. She claimed that she had never believed in God, nor had she any intention to start anytime soon. Furthermore, she stated that religious believers were a dangerous element of our society, and that she wished to assist the KGB to apprehend the leaders of the church by pointing out people and places belonging to the underground organization.

At first I could not believe what I had heard. After all, I, along with the deacon of the church, had become totally convinced of her good intentions. Now everything came tumbling down around me.

The following evening, after the people of our city had heard and seen my teacher's speeches, the believers had another secret meeting in the cave. After I pled to go with her, Mother took me along, but they would not allow me inside the cave. I could only hear some bits and pieces. One thing was entirely clear to me. The believers were now bracing themselves for new difficulties ahead.

When, on the following day, I faced my teacher in class, I saw in her eyes mockery and contempt. After the last period Zoya Vasilievna did not dismiss the class as usual. Instead she announced a special class meeting. A protracted sigh went through the classroom. Almost everyone looked quizzically toward me. And I, burning with embarrassment, felt chills go up and down my spine. But before the meeting started, the vice-principal, accompanied by three other teachers from adjacent classrooms, walked in. With them were a Young Communist Pioneer leader, a young woman who was responsible for organizing Pioneer activities at school, and another man who seemed familiar. Than I remembered that he had been the one who had shut down our church and ordered who should be arrested. My heart began to pound twice its normal rate.

The visitors took seats behind a long table placed in front of the blackboard. The meeting began when Zoya Vasilievna called me forward and made me face the class. I don't know from where it came, but I felt a surge of courage. Calmly I walked forward and confidently smiled at the familiar faces of my classmates. "Children," my teacher said, addressing the students, "I must bring to you a most unpleasant bit of news. More specifically, a student of our class, Sasha Ponomarov, who up to now has been known not only as a fine Pioneer, but as a chairman of the Pioneer group and a class president, has become a sectarian and has been constantly skipping school on Saturdays in order to attend the services of a strange Christian church."

She briefly paused, as though expecting a reaction from my classmates, and then turned toward me. With a malicious smile she said, "Tell us all, Sasha, honestly, is it not true that you have become a Christian?"

"Yes," I answered easily, "that is an absolute fact. I actually have become a Christian and do not see anything wrong with it."

For a time total silence filled the room. Then students began to giggle and look at each other, while the adults at the table began to cough and fidget in their seats. Obviously my answer did not please them. Pavel Ivanovich, the vice principal and a large, heavyset man with droopy cheeks and a shiny bald head, abruptly rose from his chair, came up to me, and began to talk with a high-pitched, monotonous tone of voice. "Do you, Sasha Ponomarov, realize that because you attend that stupid church, you have disgraced the honor of your class and the honor of our school?"

Once again a new surge of courage emboldened me. "You say

I disgraced the honor of my class? May I ask before whom and in what manner did I disgrace my school? Have I become a poor student or have I violated some school rules? In what way did I disgrace my classmates and moreover the whole school?"

Pavel Ivanovich appeared somewhat flustered. Just at that very moment the chekist who had evicted the believers from our church stepped forward from behind the table. He now joined the vice principal, yelling at me in his shrill, metallic voice. "I see, you smart-aleck, that you still don't quite understand what happened in your church recently. It seems that you insist on looking for trouble. Well, let me assure you, young man, I can cause plenty for you if you persist in being stubborn." The students thought what he said was funny and burst out laughing, not understanding either the weight or the scope of the chekist's threats.

Then he faced the class. "A few months ago, by order of the governing body of the city of Ust-Kamenogorsk, the church that Sasha Ponamarov attends was officially closed. This Christian church is connected with the American spy network and engages in underground antigovernment activities. The KGB has kept some of the members of this dangerous sect under surveillance. Soon their leaders will be tried and sent to prison along with other suspected members of this church."

He lectured for about half an hour, telling the students that religious believers were especially dangerous, because they appeared to be good people on the surface, but their aim was to subvert and convert into their sect as many people as possible. Then, in conclusion, he turned to me one more time and declared, "And to you I recommend that you sever all contacts with the Christians if you don't want to end up in court yourself." Quickly he returned to his place at the table and sat down.

The Young Pioneer leader suddenly interrupted the brief silence. In her speech, as always, she made use of well-memorized platitudes on the importance of the Pioneer organization for the proper development and happy childhood of all children. Everything she had to say we already knew by heart, having heard the phrases recited many times in the past. Then turning to me, she concluded, "Sasha, since you have admitted to be a sectarian, you are not worthy of the noble name of a Pioneer."

Again, total silence filled the room. One could have heard a pin drop. All eyes were riveted on me, waiting impatiently for what might take place. In my head resounded the words: "You are not worthy of the noble name of a Pioneer." Quickly, I untied the red kerchief around my neck and placed it on the table in front of my teacher. The class became agitated. Everyone began to fidget and whisper. Among the whispers one could hear the same question: "What's going to happen now? What's going to happen now?" Everyone considered it a great moral offense to remove the red tie of the Pioneers in such a dramatic way.

Leaping from her chair, my teacher began to tear off the red chevrons on my sleeves, the marks of honor and distinction. Every class president wore on his school uniform three red stripes to indicate his position. Now Zoya resembled a military general pulling off epaulets, the symbolic gesture used to disgrace a treasonous officer. As she did so, she hysterically mumbled, "Never again will you preside over my class, you sectarian . . ."

The next day I stood before the whole student body that had assembled to witness my expulsion from the Pioneer organization and my removal from the office of class president. The school principal, Ivan Ivanovich, pointed his finger at me and repeated the accusation. "This student disgraced our school by joining a Christian sect, which is dangerous for our Soviet society. From now on Sasha Ponomarov will be regarded as a black spot on the reputation of our school." After briefly pausing to make his point, he repeated it again and again in every variation he could think of.

Few of the students from either the upper or lower classes knew me. Not everyone was interested in what was going on. Consequently the large auditorium began to gradually fill with the drone of children's voices. Finally the principal finished with me, and everyone went to their classrooms.

In the hallway I accidentally bumped into Larissa. She now looked at me with disdain and even disgust. It was the very thing I had feared most. For a moment, while we walked alongside each other, I edged a bit closer to her, but she quickly moved further away. Then she exclaimed, "I don't love you. I hate you! Now I know why those guys beat you up. They did the right thing. You had it coming."

Then throwing one more arrogant glance, she scanned me from head to toe before dashing off to her class. Paralyzed, I remained standing in the center of the hallway.

Someone tapped me on the shoulder. I turned around and saw my teacher. Apparently she was saying something, but I was totally oblivious to it. Finally, as if from a distance I heard her bark, "Ponomarov, what's the matter with you?"

Regaining my senses, I curtly answered, "There's nothing wrong with me."

As we proceeded along the hallway to class, she said, "By the way, I want you to ask your mother if she can find out who picked up the religious books from my home one day when I was away." I could not quite understand what she meant. For a moment I even forgot Larissa.

As soon as I arrived home, I asked, "Mom, what do you know about the books disappearing from Zoya Vasilievna's home?"

Mother gave me a mysterious smile and said, "Alright, come in. Please sit down and listen carefully, I'll tell you all about it, but you mustn't tell anyone."

One of the secret meetings in the cave had conceived an interesting scheme to retrieve the Bible and books the church had given my teacher. The local congregation had a rather beautiful and imposing woman named Lyuba. Her husband was some kind of high official. She found out when Zoya Vasiliyevna would be at work and showed up at the teacher's house, dressed in the latest style and fashion.

Fortunately, Zoya Vasilievna's husband was at home. Lyuba introduced herself as Zoya's close professional friend and proceeded to explain that she too, like his wife, was preparing to present a report on radio and television against the believers and that she needed the books that the church had given Zoya. Her appearance and her performance were so convincing that the husband, without the slightest suspicion, found all of the Christian books and handed them over to Lyuba.

CHAPTER 7

THE ACCIDENT

MY MOTHER'S BACKBREAKING work eventually left her extremely ill. Her legs were constantly swollen, and large blue veins appeared and looked as if they were about to burst. I don't recall that my stepfather helped her in any way. On the contrary, he frequently came home drunk and created groundless arguments. The apartment turned into nightmarish hell. Although we children tried to help out with some of the daily chores, we did them halfheartedly.

Finally one day Mother needed an emergency operation, and she was admitted into a local hospital. Our home now became empty. Because I didn't have anyone to talk with, I decided to visit her in the hospital every evening. Sometimes I could not get the bus fare from my older sister and had to walk, which took me about an hour. One evening, not having a kopek (penny) in my pocket, I still decided to go to the hospital. It was the end of October, and the weather at that time of year was usually terrible. Often it drizzled and sometimes snowed. The day was gloomy, damp, and cold.

Caught up in my conversation with Mother, I did not even notice that it was getting dark outside and that I had to return home. Luckily, she found some money for the fare, and now I could take the bus rather then walk home.

When I stepped outside, it was already dark. But there were pedestrians everywhere, and I was not afraid. As I began to cross the street, a car without headlights came out of the darkness at a great speed headed directly toward me. It was almost impossible to see it in the darkness. In a split second it knocked me off my feet and sent me flying through the air. I hit the ground, unconscious. The vehicle sped away and disappeared in the darkness.

Thank God some kind people at the bus stop witnessed what had happened, and someone was able to write down the license plate number. The others rushed up to me. One of them quickly stopped a passing car, and they took me to the same hospital where my unsuspecting Mother lay.

The doctors quickly gave me first aid and examined me. They discovered that I had a shattered left hip, a head concussion, and many bruises. By sheer coincidence a neighbor, "Aunt Tonya," worked in the hospital as a radiologist. Luckily, she took all the X-rays and saw for herself to what extent my left hip was shattered. Aunt Tonya was an unmarried elderly woman with a stern face. It seemed to me that she never smiled.

Recognizing me right away, she told the doctor, "The boy's mother is getting treatment in the surgical ward." In just a few minutes the hospital allowed Mother to come to my ward. Seeing her 10-year-old son almost totally bandaged and unconscious, she shrank from pain and horror. From that moment on she did not leave my bedside.

After several sleepless nights and many injections, I finally began to feel better. I had already begun to talk, move, and eat. The fractured bones were gradually healing, and life again began to return to normal. Tears filled mother's eyes less frequently. Sparks of joy and hope shone through them again— that another of life's sorrows was behind her, and soon it would be possible to breathe more freely. Unfortunately, it was not to be.

At that time she was being prepared for surgery and had to return to the surgical ward. There she met a woman who suffered from untreatable leukemia. The rather young woman knew that she would die soon and almost constantly talked about it with anyone who cared to listen to her.

Forgetting her own fears, Mother decided to help the suffering woman by lending her the Bible. It so happened that the woman's husband worked with the KGB. Having seen a Bible in his wife's possession, he began to question her about it. The very next day the hospital canceled my mother's operation and released her from the hospital. When asked why they were dismissing her, the hospital answered, "For distributing religious propaganda."

When I found out what had happened, I slipped into depression. For several days I could not cope with the knowledge that religious believers in our country had absolutely no rights at all. One had to accept the fact that a Christian could receive no help.

After a few days my teacher visited me in the hospital. She said that she was sorry for my accident. However, she quickly added, not without some sarcasm, "See, Sasha, your God didn't bother to help you in this situation, did He?"

In addition, she told the doctors as well as the nurses that I was a believer and attended an underground Christian church that the government had had to shut down. For me, too, the time had come when I had to suffer not only the physical pain from broken bones and from bruises, but also from mental abuse and ridicule.

Two months after the accident, "Aunt Tonya"—our neighbor the radiologist—came to see me. Since her apartment was across the hall from ours, I had seen her hundreds of times either near the apartment house or in the corridor. She always appeared to be angry. However, a big smile now lit up her face. Her voice had genuine joy in it as she said, "Sasha, you are one lucky fellow. When they brought you into our hospital, as you know, I made the X-rays and saw myself what kind of damage your left hip sustained. I could only describe it as a bag of broken bones. And now, only two months later, when I made a new series of X-rays, your bones, by some unexplainable miracle, have practically mended perfectly. I have worked in radiology for 22 years and have not seen such rapid recovery. I congratulate you, Sasha!"

Her news confirmed my confidence in the power of prayer.

My mother had requested special prayer by the entire church, and now I had seen the answer.

After the hospital released me, I found out from Mother that the driver who had hit me would be tried in court. Several people had witnessed the accident and demanded that the guilty person be brought to justice. Before the trial, however, some strangers strongly warned my mother that she had better say in court that she had forgiven the offender and wanted all charges dropped. Further, they told her that should she refuse to do it, another car would "accidentally" run me down for good, this time finishing the job.

The trial was under the direct control of the KGB. It was not difficult to notice how the judge read the prepared statements. Besides, the judge's decision had no legal basis.

Acquitted, the guilty driver left the court smiling—as if he had not committed any crime. No one dared to protest. The eyewitnesses never showed up in court, and my frightened mother was too scared to utter a single word.

Only after the trial did we understood the true nature of the "accident." Now it was clear to us that the KGB had arranged everything. Nevertheless, we had much to be thankful for. After all, God had spared my life!

Several weeks had passed since I had left the hospital. But in spite of the occasional discomfort and a slight limp I could not sit around the house. Early one Sabbath morning Mother and I headed for the worship service.

Neither of us doubted that the KGB had placed constant surveillance on our home. Therefore, as we left our home for church, we figured that if we walked separately, we would have a greater chance of losing the agent watching us. After all, it is much harder to follow a single person than two individuals. Usually Mother left the apartment first, and after some 20 minutes, I would follow.

As I headed for the bus station, I was constantly conscious that someone was watching me. On the bus I tried to catch sight of anyone who looked in my direction more often than toward anyone else. In those days it was rare for ordinary people to own private cars. People traveled by public transportation or simply walked. Because there were always many people on the streets, it was impossible to determine who followed me. Eventually our deacon, Peter, taught me how to spot the person following me. After leaving the bus, I would walk toward the house where the service was to be held. Turning my head slightly, I could spot whoever tailed me.

According to the rules the church members had established, when I would reach the appointed house, I would turn into the neighboring street, then into another, and finally end up on the original street. In other words, I would make a complete circle, called "the circle of precaution." Then I would repeat the same route.

If I noticed anyone constantly following me, that meant that I was being watched, since no one walks the same streets just for the fun of it. In such a case I would not enter the house where the worship service was being held, but would simply return home.

This time everything seemed all right. After making two or three "circles of precaution" and not seeing anyone tailing me, I entered the house safely. Meeting the believers of our group was like being with my own family. The worshipers told each other about their daily experiences, how difficult it was for believers to keep a job, and shared their family problems.

The worship service had no singing. The deacon even preached his sermon in a semi-whisper. Just before we were dismissed, everyone knelt down for benediction. Suddenly, we heard a loud knock on the door, interrupting the prayer. The man of the house, a young person named Victor, pantomimed with his hand that we were to sit down around the table and pretend that we were eating. Victor's wife, Olga, began to pour soup into the soup dishes. In the confusion someone dropped a plate, and it crashed on the floor with a loud noise.

By now someone beat on the door with fists, and we could hear "Open the door or we'll break it into pieces!" When Victor opened it, several armed policemen rushed into the room. All of the men were huge, with square shoulders and square faces. They reminded me of walking refrigerators. "Everybody remain in your place," they barked. "Nobody move!" We all sat around the table and stared at each other. When I looked at Peter, his eyes smiled and his head gave me an encouraging nod. I nodded back, signaling that I was not afraid of anybody.

The policemen, along with two chekists, searched the rooms, looking under the beds and cupboards. Apparently they thought someone was hiding.

One of the elderly women who sat across from me, apparently to reduce tension, began to recite a Christian poem. A police officer standing behind her lifted his fist and shouted, "Shut your mouth, or I'll do it for you!"

No one could move for about an hour. By now the chekists were rummaging through drawers, boxes, the table drawers, and even the pots in the kitchen. Throwing blankets and pillows off the bed onto the floor, they kept saying, "We'll find where they keep their religious literature that they get from the United States of America."

Finally the search ended fruitlessly, and the police again gathered in the room where we sat. One of the chekists came up to the table, struck it with his fist, and, choking with fury, rasped, "Oh, if I had the power, I'd gun down everyone of you. Yes, we should get all of you into one room and finish you off."

Victor, as the host of the house, tried to explain that we were his friends and that he had invited us for dinner and not to a religious service. One of the police officers laughed sarcastically, and, looking at Victor, asked maliciously, "Then why didn't you eat anything? You people had gathered here over an hour ago. We have been watching your house for more than two hours. You believers are not supposed to lie, and don't try to make fools of us. We know exactly who is here and for what purpose."

One chekist patted the policeman on the shoulder approvingly and added, "You said the absolute truth. We know everything, and you people can't fool us. Not only can we tell you exactly what you were talking about, but be assured that we have the means at our disposal to see and hear everything that goes on."

The other police officer, standing by the door and apparently also trying to score a few points in front of the chekist, added, "Everything is known to us, not only what you say during the day, but even what you say at night in your beds." After he said this, he began to laugh. Apparently he thought his claim very funny. But no one else laughed. Guiltily looking at his comrades, he cut short his laughter and began to cough, nervously covering his mouth with his hand.

The chekist angrily stared at the people around the table. Peter looked straight into his face and calmly said, "We are ready for the time when we will be tortured and killed for Jesus Christ."

The man grimaced with loathing, threw a contemptuous look at Peter, and asked, "So you're ready to die now?"

The question startled the deacon momentarily, then regaining his composure, he said calmly and firmly, "Yes, I'm ready even now."

The chekist unbuttoned his jacket, and I saw a pistol in a holster under his arm. My whole insides turned cold. *It seems the time has come again when, just as earlier under Stalin, many believers will be shot without a trial,* I thought. Everyone in the room froze.

Then the other chekist began to button his cohort's jacket and in a joking tone said, "We won't shoot any of you today, but we'll arrest a few. The rest of you will have to give us your addresses and places of employment so we'll know what to do next."

After they had recorded our addresses in their books, the chekist looked at the deacon and ordered, "Arrest this brash fellow. I'd like to become better acquainted with him." His words had a threatening undertone to them, hinting that he would interrogate the deacon until he found out more about the congregation's internal life. Otherwise, they would hold Peter in a special cell in which they would torture him to break his will and faith.

Peter rose from his place, and two policemen took him by the arms and led him toward the police van. They also arrested Victor as the organizer of the worship service. The rest of us they ordered to return home and never gather again for worship services.

The elderly woman who tried to recite a poem asked the others quietly, "How do you think they found us out?" People offered various suggestions. Possibly one of our own members had given us away. Perhaps the neighbors had been watching us. Or someone had been careless in coming to the meeting.

We stood around a while in a circle, sighed, moaned, grumbled, then wished each other a safe trip home and departed. Now we could go to the bus stop without taking any precautions since the authorities would not be following us.

When I reached home, I tried to retrace my steps in my mind. It seemed to me that I had been quite careful and had seen no one tailing me. How the KGB found us remained a big mystery to me too.

Winter ended and spring arrived. Now completely recovered, I felt just fine.

One evening two well-dressed young men came to our apartment. By their attire they looked like teachers or office workers. They said they were from a social organization taking a census, and they wanted to talk to all the members of our family.

Their questions covered a number of topics. They asked how we liked the service in stores, did we get along with our neighbors, what did we do for entertainment, and other similar topics.

Our whole family was present. At first it appeared that they gave equal attention to each of us. But gradually they began to focus more and more on Mother and me. After the initial visit, they came around two or three other times. With each visit their questions became more demanding. They were interested in who of the believers came to see us. Did the pastor ever visit us? Did we enjoy reading religious literature? And if they themselves wanted to read such things, where could they obtain Christian books? The tone of their voices became more and more harsh.

At their last visit they behaved extremely rudely. I remember one of them telling me quite sharply, "I most firmly recommend that you forget that Christian sect if you don't want to cause your family or yourself unnecessary troubles."

Rising and staring at my mother, he added, "And to you, his mother, I suggest you exercise due influence on your son so he will develop the interests of other normal children, rejoin the Young Pioneer group, and stop attending church on Saturdays.

See to it, unless you want to have some problems at work." With that he left the room and slammed the door.

My stepfather sat on the bed, supporting his head with his hands. Without looking at me, he said, "Sasha, you are only 11 years of age and are already causing such foolishness. Don't you understand that you are ruining not only your own life but ours as well? You think they are coming to see us for no special reason? I know for sure they're going to cause much trouble for our family."

Valya, my stepsister, jumped into the conversation. "Many of my friends ask me in school, 'What's the matter with your brother? He seems so weird? Why does he have to go to that stupid church? He's already been kicked out of the Pioneer organization. Can't you, as an older sister, forbid him to attend that church?' "

My stepbrother had sat there in silence, just drawing some lines on paper. Hearing all this, he sighed heavily and said, "I hate all this mess. I can't understand, Sasha, why you can't just live peacefully? Believe in your heart all you want to but don't let anybody know about it, and everything will be just fine. . . . Is it that hard to understand?"

He wanted to say something else, but Mother stirred by the table and said in a cheerful voice, "I think the most important thing right now is to have a good dinner. And now you're all invited to the table." That ended the awkward conversation.

Two or three days later the kindergarten director where Mother had worked for many years invited her into her office for a chat. The director was by nature a kind woman. She told my mother that she had been called before the "Conformity" department, another name for the KGB. There they had ruthlessly quizzed her. "Do you know that a sectarian is working in your department?"

"Yes, I know that Nina is a Christian," she had replied.

"And why do you still keep her at work?"

My mother's supervisor had tried to defend her. "Because Nina is a good worker. She has worked here for many years, and there hasn't been a single complaint about her. And our whole staff is happy with her performance."

"We're giving you two days to get rid of her," they ordered. "If not, we'll fire you and take your membership from the Communist Party. Do you understand? Now go and do as you're told!"

With that the director fired Mother. No further explanation was necessary. And now our family had lost my mother's regular though modest income. It meant that unless our friends or some kind people helped us, we would be unable to buy needed food. My stepfather spent almost all of his earnings on alcohol, and we could not depend on his earnings. Dismissed workers did not receive assistance from the government.

The next evening the same two young men came to our apartment. One of them said to Mother, "You didn't want to comply with our recommendations, and that's why you lost your job. And since your apartment belongs to the government organization where you were employed, you must vacate it by tomorrow."

She began to cry and pled for more time to locate another place to live in. To find another apartment in those days was practically impossible. But the men shook their heads and coldly stated, "We cannot do a thing about it. This problem is of your own making, it was your choice." With that they left.

My stepfather was furious, shouting at Mother and at me. It turned into an extremely bad evening for our family. But still no one believed that we would be evicted.

The next morning my stepfather went to work as usual, and Mother stayed at home with us children. The schools had already closed for summer vacation. At about 10:00 in the morning the same two men returned to our apartment. By now I knew for sure they were KGB agents. With them they brought three other men in work clothes. They told us to vacate the apartment immediately. Mother tried to maintain her composure. "Show me the legal papers that say we must leave," she said.

The chekists burst into laughter. "Tomorrow, my dear lady, we'll bring you the documents you want," one of them said, "even with a pretty seal on them. But for now get out of here immediately or we'll toss you out like garbage."

It was quite clear that they were capable of doing anything. Then Mother, turning to us, said, "Children, it seems we have no choice but to move out on the street." She left the room first. Then we, giving each other quizzical looks, followed suit. We could not grasp what had just transpired.

The laborers from the KGB began to carry out our possessions and toss them into the street. As they threw our clothing through the window, we picked it up, shook off the dust, and folded it into one pile. They hurled out our school briefcases with our notebooks and textbooks, our old soccer ball, and our big kite that my brother and I had constructed just a few days before.

Although we felt like crying, shouting, and even fighting with them, we had to resign ourselves to the fact that we were helpless and could do nothing about it. Several neighbors, home at the time and hearing the commotion, came out—first into the hallway and then outside—to see what was happening. They really could not understand what was going on.

I remember that several of them demanded, "What are you doing? Why are you evicting this fine family?" Some neighbors, seeing Mother crying and us staring at everything with frightened eyes, tried to prevent the men from tossing our things. The chekists began to shove them rudely aside and threatened to punish them harshly if they interfered in someone else's business.

One brave elderly neighbor had gone through the war as a soldier and was not afraid of anybody or anything. Seeing my mother crying and how we children cowered in the corner, he attempted to stop the men from ejecting our things into the street. The chekists immediately pushed him away and threatened him if he continued to interfere with the law and what was none of his business.

I saw one of the chekists run to his vehicle and radio for help. In a few minutes or so another car arrived in front of our apartment building. Several huge police officers filed out of the car, and one of them roared, "Who of you is trying to interfere with the authority here?"

The neighbors quickly dispersed and returned to their apartments. We could hear how they locked their doors behind them. Again we were left alone.

Terrified, I thought, *Why are these things happening? Why do these trials follow one after another?* My stepsister looked at me indignantly and blurted, "And it's all because of you! . . . It's all your fault!"

Meanwhile Mother didn't just sit there. She bustled about in a shed behind the building. I don't know where she got the whitewash. All I remember is that toward evening she had transformed the shed into a small room. She had painted the inside walls of the shed and hung our pictures and clock on the walls, just as in our previous apartment. We carried in our beds. With difficulty we squeezed in our dining table, over which Mother hung a small cupboard for the dishes. The decorative rugs covered the wall above our beds. She even found room for our clothes cabinet. On the floor lay our familiar mats.

It seemed to me that Mother had performed a miracle, and now the old, ugly shed resembled our former apartment, except that it was a bit smaller. To this day I do not cease to wonder how this sick woman summoned the energy for such hard work and still be cheerful.

To add to our problems, she now also had to look for work. Every day Mother went to various organizations in search of a job. At that time the country had a great labor shortage, yet she could not find employment anywhere. At first they would tell her, "We certainly need workers, and we would be glad to give you work." But no sooner did she show them her passport, as required by law, than they recognized her name, and the tune immediately changed. "We're sorry, but we cannot hire you. Goodbye." Mother went to one organization after another and continued to hear the same story. Only once did some brave person tell her, "Woman, give up looking for work. Your name is known everywhere, and every place has orders not to hire you."

Finally, realizing that looking for work in government-run organizations was useless, Mother decided to contact the more affluent. She offered to do any kind of work for any kind of pay. And so she went to the large attractive apartments near us.

Ordinarily, KGB staff, directors of factories and business firms, and other managers lived in such homes. All Communists, they proclaimed high ideas and beautiful slogans about equality among all people.

Meanwhile, the authorities warned us that the shed too belonged to the government and that we had to leave immediately. Five years earlier our stepfather had constructed another shed from plywood to store firewood and charcoal. Again Mother performed a miracle. Of course our portable closet now stood sideways at the entrance, and we could use it only after we opened the shed door.

As children we did not see our situation as a problem. After all, every morning, as before, we received our breakfast. Then, after we did our simple chores, we spent our time playing games, forgetting our difficulties. But it was quite a different matter for our parents. Their life had changed considerably. My stepfather announced that he wanted a divorce, since, as he expressed himself, a "dog's life" did not suit him. "Be patient a bit longer," Mother begged, "and everything will be normal again."

Eventually, with great difficulty, Mother found work, cleaning several homes and earning alms' wages. But it helped.

Luckily, we located the grandmother of my half-siblings, Valya and Ivan. During the summer they went to live with her. I was told that the woman was their father's mother, and since I was not her blood relative, I was not welcome. I understood that I had no place to go for the summer, and I had better get used to things the way they were.

Every day I went to the shed as to my regular home. Even the scornful glances and sarcastic remarks from my neighborhood friends about our "plush" living accommodations came to be a normal state of affairs. Two months flew by. Autumn was approaching, and it became necessary to look for real shelter.

During that period of history our country had a law on the books that guaranteed a roof over the heads of the relatively small number of people lucky enough to own even a small house of their own. But the largest segment of our society did not have the means for the most ordinary things of life, much less purchase a house or an apartment. They were content after years of waiting to be allowed to move into a government-built apartment complex. But until then the workers' families had to huddle together the best they could. And even when finally they received "their" apartment, another law allowed the government the right to evict and take the apartment back and give it to someone else. Because our family's government apartment had no guarantee of permanent occupancy, the authorities simply tossed us out on the street like garbage.

Fortunately, our church deacon Peter had a neighbor, an older woman, who lived in her own house. While she was not a believer, still she was a kind person and decided to help us out. She took us in on the condition that we assist her with her vegetable garden and with home chores and repairs. Loading our meager belongings on a small truck furnished by another kind neighbor, we moved into our new home.

However, we stayed no more than two weeks in our new place, when our new landlord told us that some officials quickly warned her that if she continued to allow us to live with her, she would have a lot of trouble. "Furthermore," they said, "these people are sectarians and belong to an outlawed Christian church that has ties with the American spy network. They are very dangerous people to have anything to do with, so as soon as possible, get them out of your house!"

She did so without delay.

Just about that time, though, another Christian family had moved from the country into our town. They had recently purchased their own home and agreed to give us shelter in their house, offering us one room and a small kitchen to share. Again, packing our few belongings, we moved into yet another part of town.

CHAPTER 8

"GOD IS NOT MOCKED"

ANOTHER SUMMER FLEW BY, a child's best part of the year. And again autumn arrived with its school responsibilities and worries.

That fall I went to another school located closer to our home. It felt like a new beginning with a new school, new teachers, and new students in my class. But I still worried that after a while here too, I would not be able to avoid the mockery and torment that I had endured in the previous one.

Apparently no one knew about me as yet, and that accounted for the good attitude of teachers and students alike toward me. I became good friends with some boys from my class. More than a month of peaceful, happy school days went by. But one Monday the school principal called me into his office.

Ivan Petrovich in many respects resembled the principal of the previous school. Average in height, round-shouldered, he had glasses with lenses that made his eyes appear unusually small. He too was a chain smoker, and his face had the same yellowish tinge. His yellow, widely set teeth reminded me of a row of old stumps.

His office was just as uninviting, messy, and even as gloomy as the former principal's. Thick, dark drapery tightly covered the window, and no ray of sunshine could penetrate into the room. On one wall hung an oversized portrait of Lenin that occupied nearly half of the space and gave the room an overwhelming and highly political atmosphere.

When I walked in, the principal remained seated and, pointing to an empty chair, motioned me to sit down. The "interview" began with Petrovich lighting a new cigar. He inhaled a lung-full of smoke, then exhaled it in small circles, and began talking to me with a drawl without looking in my direction. "The appropriate department informed me who you are, and why you moved into this part of town. I want you to know, Sasha, that I know more about you than you might suppose."

Pausing, he then produced from his drawer a sheet of paper and began to attentively study it. Then suddenly remembering that he had someone in his office, he made another prolonged draw on his cigar, blowing out tiny white clouds from his mouth, and decided to continue his monologue.

Speaking rapidly yet haltingly, he only occasionally glanced in my direction. I felt that even when he did look at me, he didn't see me. Suddenly he rose from behind the table and approached the huge portrait of Stalin. Poking his finger at it, he said in a loud, proud voice, "There is my god. He gave me bread, shelter, education, and everything that I needed. . . . But your God in heaven cannot give me anything no matter what or how much I ask Him."

I felt the urge to argue, but I changed my mind and thought to myself, *Anything I say might infuriate him. It would be better if I remain silent just as I did in my previous school.*

The very next Monday, following my absence on Saturday, the director summoned me again. My weekly treks to the principal's office continued for some time. Ivan Petrovich talked with me usually for an hour or even an hour and a half at a time. But one could not say that we really had a conversation since he did all the talking. The only time he paused was to take a breath or to inhale another puff of smoke. Otherwise, he charged on nonstop the whole time, as if he shot the words from a machine gun.

Occasionally he called me some choice names, such as a

blockhead, a circular idiot (honestly to this very day I can't figure that one out), and gave me other most exotic wild and domestic animal's names. At times it even seemed to me that he loved animals, and that was why he so often referred to them. On the other hand, it appeared as if he hated the creatures, because he referred to me and all the believers by their names. As I left his office, I often thought, *Maybe Ivan Petrovich is sick and perhaps I should pray for him.*

One Monday as I headed to my routine appointment with the principal, I had to pass through the faculty room. As I entered I saw several teachers sitting or standing around a long table. Apparently they were getting ready for the next class. The principal was there too. Seeing me, he smiled broadly and, pointing to me with his hand, said so that everybody could hear, "Look here, the prophet of God has come." The teachers burst into laughter. "Tell us, Sasha, isn't it true that soon there will take place a judgment on us atheist teachers."

When I answered only with an affirmative nod, everybody exploded in another round of obscene laughter. I heard someone exclaim, "So young and he already believes such nonsense." Then the principal again took another long puff on his cigarette, looked about the room with obvious self-satisfaction, and explained to the assembled teachers as he exhaled the smoke, "Christians have the notion that very soon their Christ will return and take them all to heaven, but we all shall stay here and just burn." Then he turned to me and asked, "How old are you?"

"Twelve," I answered.

"And I am 56. For your information, I've been sinning all my life, yet I'm not afraid of any God. And I'm convinced that no one will ever punish me for my sins. But if I should violate our Soviet laws, then they'll punish me—that is, if they catch me. But for 'sins' there is no punishment, trust me!"

Then he lifted both of his hands upward and, trying to appear as ridiculous as possible, shouted, "Oh God, if You exist, please punish me." More laughter filled the room. The principal looked at me one more time, waved his hand, and gruffly shouted, "Get out, 'Man of God,' and stop entertaining us."

The next day when I came to school I encountered the vice principal in the hallway. The tall, but full-figured woman with brightly painted lips and heavily powdered face usually ignored the students around her. Today, however, she actually greeted me. Stunned, I could not understand why.

At the door to our classroom I met two of my friends. Agitated expressions on their faces, they grabbed me by my shoulders and started tugging me in all directions. "Sasha," they shouted, "now no one will bother you on Mondays anymore, because . . ."

Each one of them urgently tried to tell me some important news, but they only interrupted each other, and I could not sort out what they were saying. Again I heard one of them announce, "Now they'll leave you in peace, because . . ."

"What happened?" I demanded impatiently.

But they continued talking with such excitement that they were almost incoherent. Finally I heard the terrible news. "The principal hanged himself during the night!"

I found it difficult to believe my ears. But when the school's PA system announced over the loudspeakers that school would be closed for the day due to the principal's death, I had absolutely no reason for doubt.

Now, in a strange sort of way, I understood the vice principal's friendly greeting at the door. But, most significantly, perhaps this tragic news, in light of what had happened in the faculty room the previous day, was the most important lesson of my life: "God is not mocked."

Meanwhile, unbeknown to our family, the KGB was gathering material to use against us in court. Firing Mother from work and evicting us from the apartment had not satisfied them. Now they were manufacturing evidence that they could employ to accuse Mother of violating Soviet laws. But not suspecting a thing, we children focused on our school work, and our parents worried about finding enough money to somehow survive.

The New Year holidays were over. Of course this year we were unable to purchase even the least expensive presents.

That's why we were busily making some handmade gifts to give each other for the traditional New Year event.

January had arrived—the coldest month of the year. The winter that year was severe. Snowdrifts covered everything. The people only cleared narrow paths or stomped tracks through the snow. Road crews could not keep up with clearing the streets from the snow, and vehicles moved slowly on the bumpy roads. But I loved this time of the year, when I could ski and sled to my heart's content—or simply wallow in the snow until someone would say, "Hey, you, your nose turned white. I bet it's frost-bitten." Dashing home, I would let Mother massage it or rub something on it until it resumed it's normal pink again. Then I would run outside again as if nothing had happened.

Preoccupied with games and snowball fights with the neighborhood boys, I had completely forgotten all that I had gone through. But I would have only a short reprieve.

The regional newspaper, *Rudniy Altay* (The Mining Altay), soon printed an article under the heading, "Endangered Child." In it the author told how a boy named Sasha Ponomarov had fallen prey to the dangerous influence of a Christian sect, and unless he received immediate help, the believers would offer him up as a sacrifice or do something equally terrible to him. The article ended with a plea: "Communist citizenry ought to help Sasha immediately and free him from the influence of his sectarian mother, who is crippling his personality with her religious biases, making the boy kneel by the hour day and night reading the Bible."

The only thing accurate in the story was my name and my address, but we had no way to rebut it and tell the readers the truth. The KGB could print in newspapers and books whatever they deemed necessary to advance Communism. But no other person had the right to present any other perspective. Thus the majority of people in our country blissfully accepted whatever the government wanted them to believe. Almost every day we heard on the radio a popular song that declared, "I know of no such other country in the world, where a person can breath as freely as here."

Three days after the publication of the newspaper article, a television crew and reporters came to our house. Flashbulbs exploded and movie cameras followed our every move. They were filming for a bizarre kind of novelty show about a boy sectarian who skipped school to go to church on Saturdays.

Of course I was not prepared for their invasion and did not know how to respond. I remember that the correspondent—a tall, handsome elderly man with a pleasant voice—asked me many unexpected questions. "Do you, Sasha, consider yourself a happy person? Does your mother restrict your rights? Have you been told, Sasha, that your father is not actually your real father?"

Each time I tried to think of an answer or made a serious face, the operator of the camera zeroed in on my face and the reporter commented to the audience, "Just look at this unfortunate boy. He never smiles. Can you believe it, Christians are actually forbidden to laugh? They consider this to be a great, unpardonable sin."

The next evening the television program "Novosti" (News) presented a "sensational" piece on how a 12-year-old boy had become a Christian. "Imagine," the commentator said, "all of this happened in our time, after our Soviet cosmonauts have gone into space and did not find any God there. When we have split the atom. . . . When we can cause rain where there is a lack of it. . . . When we ourselves have become as gods. . . . To believe in the existence of a God in our time is not only ludicrous, it is stupid." The show ended with the usual appeal: "We communists must save Sasha from the clutches of Christian influence and turn him into a happy communist."

It was but the first step in the KGB's plans.

About a week later my parents received an official summons to appear before a judge. During his conversation with my parents, the official warned them that he had sufficient evidence against them to try Mother as a criminal. "I'm giving you two weeks to think about it," he told her. "If your son, Sasha, during this time will start attending school on Saturdays, I promise to close this case without a trial. But if he is not in school on Saturdays, then you'll have no one but yourselves to blame."

That evening seemed dark and foreboding. Even the blinding,

sparkling white snow and familiar happy voices of the neighbor-hood kids outside my window could not ease my tension and de-pression. I knew something terrible was about to happen.

Despite her conversation with the judge, Mother tried to maintain an air of calm and cheerfulness when we reached home. But I noticed new worry-wrinkles in the corners of her eyes. She even forgot to take her coat off when she came into the house, even though it was adequately warm inside.

My stepfather had a quick snack and went directly to bed without saying a word. Then, while my stepsister and step-brother were still playing outside, Mother and I talked. She told me about her conversation with the judge. Suddenly she became animated and said, "You know what, Sasha, the judge's face seemed very familiar to me. But I cannot exactly recall where I have met the person."

Then her expression again grew sad and she gently embraced me, gave me an affectionate squeeze, and said almost in a whis-per, "I don't want to part with you, my son."

Not understanding, I jumped up and asked, "What are you talking about, Mother?"

She took both of my arms into her warm hands and, looking into my eyes, said softly, "They want to indict me in order to take you away from me. . . . Do you understand?"

Leaping from my seat and waving my hands, I exclaimed, "It will never happen! They can't do it!"

Mother sat motionless. Looking me squarely in the eyes, she said, "Believe me, they can do anything they want to."

Suddenly we heard a soft knock. When Mother opened the door, I saw the pastor of our church. His visit, as never before, was very timely. Quickly he assured Mother that he had stopped by just for a few minutes, no more than 10. His pleasant smile and peaceful demeanor relaxed us. Even his sparse red hair, which I had never liked before, seemed attractive.

Sitting close to me, he asked softly, "How are you doing, Sasha?"

"Everything seems all right for now," I replied. "What will happen next I have no idea."

Pastor Demko again smiled and said, "The most important thing, Sasha, is to keep in mind that God is with us always no matter what, that He loves each one of us. And please, Sasha, try to understand and remember that God will never allow any trials or problems to come your way that you cannot bear. Remember, everything that will happen to you, you will be able to endure. Because the Bible says so."

Mother briefly told the pastor about her conversation with the judge and about the scheduled trial date. His face becoming extremely serious, he placed his arm on my shoulder and said, "The whole church is praying for you. We know that you are going through difficult times. I promise you that on the day of your trial, church members will fast and fervently pray for you. And now before I go, I would like to pray with you." We knelt down and the pastor prayed.

After the prayer the pastor left just as unexpectedly as he had arrived. But his presence seemed to linger like the perfume of flowers. I felt ready for whatever might happen.

The following Sabbath we had a short worship service. Only five people attended. But it was a pleasant time of Bible study and sincere prayer.

Two weeks went by. The Monday of the third week we found in our mailbox the court summons, an official document with the government emblem and a seal on it. I held the document of thick paper with my trembling hands and read on it: "Ponomarov, Nina, and her son, Sasha, are ordered to appear before the court . . . ," followed by the address and time of the appointed trial.

Like a flock of black ravens many questions flew into my head. *So the trial will take place after all. That means something horrible awaits me. But I don't think they can put me in jail—I'm not an adult yet. Could perhaps something still be done to avert the crisis . . . ¿*

Mother took a seat beside me and asked in a kidding tone, "Is my hero very much afraid of the court?"

I tried to respond in kind. "I'm not afraid of the court, it's the verdict that I'm scared of."

The day of the trial had arrived.

The morning of the appointed day my stepfather's face was very gloomy. In fact, he did not speak to me at all. My stepbrother and stepsister also tried to avoid me, and if they did say anything, it was only a few words of mockery. Only Mother attempted to be cheerful. She ironed a white shirt for me and prepared my best suit that I wore only for worship services or special occasions.

Mother also put on her best dress and looked rather festive. Just before we had to leave, she asked me, "Do you know, Sasha, how the early Christians went to their death during the time of Roman persecution?" I shook my head, not quite understanding why she would pose such a question.

"When the Christians were sent to the arena to be torn apart by wild beasts, or to be burned at the stake, they usually put on white robes as a symbol of their purity before God and people," she answered.

Quickly I glanced at my white shirt and then at her white blouse and muttered with some trepidation, "I hope we're not going to be put to death today, are we?"

Near the courthouse we met several believer-friends from our church. They told us that in order to enter the courtroom, people had to show their passports. And since their passports were stamped "believer," the authorities would not allow them in. Oh how I wished to see the face of our pastor in the courtroom. I felt that he certainly could have prompted me what to say or help me some other way.

At the entrance to the courtroom a guard asked Mother to show him her passport. When he saw Mother's name, he awkwardly asked, "So you're on trial today?" Mother nodded decisively, took me by the hand, and just as decisively walked in. Once inside, she scanned the room, looking for a place to sit. The guard that had met us at the entrance followed her and explained that she could not sit just anywhere, that she had a special place at the bench reserved for the accused.

A few minutes later three other guards approached us. They all were just about the same height, wearing the same bright-red militia uniforms, and to me they all looked alike. Turning to my mother, one of them asked, "Are you Ponomarova, Nina?"

"Yes, I am," she answered calmly.

"Then follow me," and we all went to the front row of the courtroom. On the other side of the bar, on the raised platform, we saw a sign: "The bench of the accused." The guard stopped and pointed with his hand to the sign. "Your place is here for now." Mother hesitated for a moment, then taking control of herself, sat down. The guard brought a chair for me and placed it behind the dock, then turned around and said, "Your place will be here today, beside your Mother. Sit down!"

I began to shiver from tension and apprehension. Everything appeared to me a bit blurred and indistinguishable. The people seemed to be behind a veil of fog, and their voices blended into a meaningless drone. It all seemed a nightmare from which I desperately wanted to awaken.

People took their seats. The noise in the courtroom gradually died down. I cannot say how many people were in the room exactly—maybe 100. I only remember that it was filled. Gradually I calmed down and began to examine a long table at the front of the raised platform. Behind that table were several chairs with high backs carved with Soviet seals. Behind and above the table in a red frame hung a huge portrait of Lenin. The room had no windows, and all sorts of communist slogans covered the walls, summoning the Soviet people to mobilize their energies in pursuit of communist ideals.

Suddenly a door behind the table flung open, and into the courtroom filed several men dressed in dark suits. The bailiff, a tall person with a shiny, bald head who led the procession, shouted, "Rise! The court is in session!" Everybody stood to their feet.

Three people approached the table. In the center was the judge flanked by two court assessors. The court assessors, or "People's Representatives," were ordinary individuals selected by the people for a term of one or two years. Their function consisted of controlling the court proceedings during the court session. As a rule, the assessors were mere passive observers who unconditionally placed their signatures under the already predetermined decisions of the court.

On the left side of the judge rested a table for the defense lawyer. However, on this day there was no one there. On the right of the judge was a table for the prosecutor. He had all the evidence against the defendant, which he had to present before the court. To one side of the prosecutor stood another table. Behind it sat the two chekists who had driven the believers from our church and who had arrested the pastor.

When everyone rose to their feet, I suddenly saw Mother's face. She turned toward me, but since she could not say anything, gave me an encouraging nod. I responded with a wave of my hand and nodded back. The guard who stood next to me bent over and sternly ordered, "Now your mother has no right to look around. She has to look only at the judge."

Apparently the guard beside Mother was saying the same thing to her. The bald-headed bailiff shouted, "You may be seated!" Everybody sat down, and a tomblike silence fell over the room. In the total silence I felt as if I was among some robots, each of which performed its preprogrammed function. And hidden somewhere lurked the person who manipulated each of the robots as in a game.

Then the loud, monotonous voice of one of the court assessors interrupted the silence as he began to read the names of all those who presided before the day's proceedings. When I heard the name of Vladimir Dryapochkin, I involuntarily shuddered. I could not believe my ears. It was the same judge who two years ago had tried the driver who had run me down with his car. His thick, black wavy hair graying at the temples, his big hooked nose, and his equally black sideburns testified of his non-Russian origin, even though his name was Russian. At the previous trial Mother and I had been the victims, but now we were the defendants.

Apparently he did not recognize either Mother or me. And maybe court procedure would not allow him to reveal his inner feelings if any. The prosecutor, a stocky man of about 50 with an unnaturally red face and a large wart on the tip of his nose, proceeded to read his list of accusations: "Citizen Nina Ponomarov was drawn in to a very dangerous Christian sect. She in turn enticed her son Sasha to join it. On several occasions

131

she was seen at the forbidden, illegal worship services along with her son, an act that our country's laws categorically forbid. Every Saturday her son Sasha regularly cuts school in flagrant disregard of school discipline. Sasha is no longer active in school and has begun to study poorly . . ."

As the prosecutor continued reading, I thought, *Is it possible that all these lies could convict an innocent person ¿*

Finally the long list of accusations ended. The bailiff shouted again, "Defendant Nina, rise!" Mother stood up and attentively peered into the judge's face. It seemed that she too recognized him.

The judge posed the first question. "Defendant Ponomarov, Nina, do you plead guilty to these charges¿"

"Guilty¿ Of what¿" Mother asked.

The judge spread his arms and continued. "Guilty of violating the Soviet laws that forbid anyone to attend illegal worship services and to take minor children to religious meetings. And this is what you are being tried for today."

"In that case," she replied, "why not make it legal so we could gather openly for our Bible studies and allow us to pray and worship our God¿"

One of the chekists who sat beside the prosecutor jumped to his feet and said through his laughter, "It is not the function of this court to give permission for conducting worship services. So, defendant, you are misdirecting your requests and totally out of order."

His smooth-shaved face with its thick sagging lips and dark, tiny, mouse-like eyes repulsed me. Even his pressed suit and his spotless white shirt did not add any measure of dignity to his personality. His conduct and his outward appearance reflected only power and self-satisfaction. Remaining on his feet, the chekist—without any direction from the judge—began to interrogate Mother. "How many years have you been a member of the Adventist sect¿"

Answer: "I was born into an Adventist family."

Chekist: "Has your sect been in existence that long here¿ Do you know that the worldwide center of your church is in the U.S.A.—in Washington¿"

Answer: "Yes, I am aware of it."

Chekist: "That means you know that your church maintains connections with the aggressive, hostile, capitalistic country of America? And knowing all this you nevertheless remained a member of this sect?"

Answer: "I very much wish that the center of our church were in Moscow. Unfortunately that is impossible . . ."

The prosecutor asked permission to speak. "Defendant, do you plead guilty to the charge of maiming your son Sasha's personality? That he is denied the joy of normal childhood and the happy companionship of his friends in school?"

"Yes, it is very difficult for my son in school, but only because the school principal portrayed him before the student body as a black spot on the school's reputation. Is he less diligent in completing his school assignments? And the fact that teachers give him poor grades is not because of his performance, but because the way this game is played."

The people in the courtroom became restless in their seats and started asking each other questions. "Silence! Silence!" the bailiff shouted.

The other chekist jumped up from his seat, raised both of his arms, and shouted angrily, "Explain yourself, Ponomarov? Do you suggest that all teachers are liars?"

"I didn't say that. I asked the principal and the teachers to assign my son extra work in all subjects for Saturdays, but they didn't. If they had done that, they would have seen if he lacked in anything. His class has students who do poor work in class and miss school more often. But why does no one drag their parents to court?"

The chekist shoved both of his hands into his pockets and, squinting his already tiny eyes, said in his metallic voice, "You are to speak for yourself and not to accuse others. You are to answer the questions directly, and not to add to it anything you want to. Is that understood?"

The judge asked to bring in the witnesses. My former teacher Zoya Vasiliyevna entered. The judge asked her, "What do you know about defendant Ponomarov?"

It was evident that it was not easy for Zoya Vasiliyevna to speak, but taking control of herself, she began, "I have known this woman for a number of years. I think Nina was a good person until she got herself involved with that sect. Several months ago she tried to ensnare me into her church and took me to their illegal worship services. Sasha was then an exemplary student and even a class president. He used to study well, but after he began to skip school on Saturdays and attend that church, his grades fell sharply. Therefore, I consider that it would be better for Sasha to live away from his mother, and I am asking the court that Ponomarov, Nina, should be deprived of her maternal rights." After her presentation, she quickly left the room through a side door.

The court summoned another witness. This time it was my teacher from the new school. A woman of about 35, she was short and slender with large blue eyes and an open, kind face. When asked the same question, "What do you know about the defendant, Nina Ponomarov, and her son Sasha?" she seemed unsure and tried to explain that she did not know either me or my mother very well. Then the thick-lipped chekist posed her a direct question. "Do you agree that Sasha should be taken away from Nina?"

My new teacher by nature was a gentle, kindhearted person, and not wishing to participate in the trial, once more reminded the court that she had not known me well enough to answer the question. The chekist cut her off sharply and asked again with his voice raised, "Answer yes or no. Do you agree with the court's decision to strip Nina of her maternal rights?"

The teacher squeezed her tiny hands and forced herself to say, "Yes, I go along with the court's decision."

Then the chekist returned to his seat and mumbled, "Well, that's more like it. If you agree, that's good."

The judge summoned the next witness. It seemed that a sub-poena had gone out to the principal of my new school. Obviously the judge did not know that the man, an ardent Communist, had committed suicide. But no one dared to explain why the director was not in court as ordered.

To cover the embarrassing situation, the prosecutor again asked to speak. "I have a few questions to ask Sasha." Then turning to me, he said, "Tell us please, is it lawful according to your God's law to work on Saturdays or not?"

I tried to recall everything that I had heard in the sermons about the Sabbath and answered, "Kind deeds we can do on the Sabbath, but we can't work."

"Does that mean that work is not a kind deed? What about playing soccer? Is it lawful?"

"No."

"How about buying something in the store on Saturday?"

"No."

Rolling his eyes, the prosecutor sneered, "That means that on Saturdays you can only read the Bible and loaf all day!" After coughing into his fist, he turned to my mother. "Defendant Ponomarov, on whose soil do you live?"

"On God's earth."

"No! You live on Soviet soil. Whose bread do you eat and whose water do you drink?" Not waiting for the answer, he raised his index finger upward and snapped, "Water, bread, and everything else that surrounds you—all of it belongs to the Soviets. And you should be grateful for it, not to your God, but to your country. Understand?

"Ponomarov, you are not being tried for believing in your God, or for praying to Him. Our country's constitution guarantees the freedom of religion to all its citizens. We are trying you for violating Soviet laws."

Communism sought to convince the majority of people that religious believers in our country had complete religious freedom, and that the government prosecuted them only for breaking the laws. In her poem the young Russian poetess, Tanya Khotkevich, had expressed the true predicament of Christians in our country when she had penned:

"You may pray to God in freedom,
But . . . God alone should hear your prayer.

For it she had received 10 years in prison.

The chekist next hurled a barrage of questions at Mother:

Where was the pastor of our church? When had she seen him last? Where did believers get their religious publications from? To whom do they give or send their offerings? And so on. The KGB agents wanted to make it appear as if the chekists had stumbled upon a special opportunity to elicit from Mother some information they needed, and they were not about to lose it.

But I remember that my Mother answered in a way that avoided any direct answers.

The court session dragged on. Additional witnesses came from the kindergarten at which Mother had once worked. Two or three more represented the apartment house we had been evicted from. I remember one of them was an alcoholic, who almost every day was drunk and beat his wife and little daughter. The police had hauled him off to jail on several occasions for rowdy behavior. Now they had called him as a witness for the prosecution. In his smoking-damaged and hoarse voice he demanded that Mother be stripped of her maternal rights and that I should be sent as far away as possible.

Finally the judge turned to the audience in the courtroom. "Perhaps someone in the audience would like to address the court?"

As if on command one young woman, seated in the very front row, jumped to her feet and began to speak rapidly, waving her arms about, without taking a breath. It seemed as if she recited a speech that someone had prepared for her beforehand. "As we understand, the boy Sasha is being held captive by his mother and this sect, and we Communists need to set him free from these sectarians. And so I ask the court that Nina Ponomarov be deprived of her maternal rights. I not only ask it, I demand it from this court!"

No sooner did she sit down then an older man with a stentorian voice, from the same row, snapped as if to attention like a soldier and rattled off something almost word for word the same. Suddenly in the back of the hall I heard a familiar voice. Looking around, I saw to my surprise Lyuba from our church. The same woman who had managed to retrieve the Christian books from my teacher's house.

A question flashed into my mind: *How in the world did she get past the guards?* The authorities permitted no believer into the courtroom. But she was here, and for me it was a happy miracle.

Her voice rang out with precision and feeling. She spoke in a measured tone, weighing every word. "Honorable judge, prosecutor, assessors, and all present, today a Christian mother is on the trial.

"I want to ask the court once more, what is this woman's crime? Her son Sasha does not smoke, or drink, or steal, or misbehave, or do anything that brings disgrace to our society. I ask you again, what is this woman being tried for? Why doesn't our country prosecute mothers who are alcoholics and prostitutes, whose children, without any supervision, sleep in basements and in the attics of public buildings? Why don't they try the parents of the neglected children who smoke, drink, and rob people in the streets and in the stores? We are afraid to leave our homes."

Suddenly the thick-lipped chekist rushed from behind the table, forgetting that everyone could see him, and shouted at the guard, "Why was this Christian allowed inside the courtroom? You should be demoted for violating orders!"

Most of the audience acted as if shocked by Lyuba's speech. Other voices echoed her question. "That's right, what is this woman being tried for?" In this brief moment people for once had heard some logical questions that they had never dared to ponder before. Then, as if someone had pressed a button, a few people began to shout communist slogans. "Sectarians are the enemies of the people!" "Believers are an obstacle to progress, to a brighter future in our communist society!" "All Christians should be removed from our Soviet society!" It was not hard to see that they had been planted in the courtroom, instructed how to act, what to say, when and how to say it.

A bell rang from the judge's table, restoring order in the court. When passions had subsided and the room became quiet, the prosecutor got up again and, attempting to regain control over the awkward scene, commented, "Today's court session has made it obvious that Ponomarov, Nina, really deserves to be deprived of her maternal rights to her son. Such is not only the opinion of the prosecutor, but the consensus of all present—witnesses as well as people in the audience.

"Therefore, examining the facts that clearly are in violation of Soviet law and taking under advisement the demands of the people who plainly expressed their views, I as a government prosecutor, ask the court to give the defendant a most severe sentence! This trial should serve as an example to the rest of the believers and put them on notice that the city of Ust-Kamenogorsk will not tolerate such behavior and disregard of the law."

After a short pause, the bailiff rose to his feet and announced, "The last word is offered to the defendant."

Now I heard my Mother's even, confident voice, "Allow me, your honors the Prosecutor and Court Assessors, to make a request. Please, I beg you, don't take my son away from me. A mother's heart could not survive such a separation. As a mother, I promise to raise my son Sasha to become an exemplary and worthy citizen of our country."

Her voice cracked for a moment, then she took hold of herself and added, "I beg of you, honorable judge, do not take away my son from me. For me, he is the thread of life, my reason for living." She sat down, buried her face into her hands, and wept silently.

The judge rose to his feet. The rest followed suit, and I heard, "The court will take a recess for consultation." It meant that the judge, the prosecutor, the assessor, and mainly the representatives from the KGB, would quickly determine the sentence.

The audience began to leave the hall through the side doors. My mother had to remain in her seat until the end of the court session. I too got up and went into the hallway and then outside.

Lyuba approached me. On her face I noticed an encouraging smile, but tears filled her eyes. Hugging me, she said, "Sasha, please don't be afraid of them. God, who is with us, is stronger than the devil, who is with them." Then she took me aside and almost in a whisper quickly added, "I need to explain something else to you, Sasha. During the whole process they didn't make one reference to a single criminal law that your mother had violated. There is no law by which to try you for believing in God or for attending worship services. The trial is based on nothing but lies. The judge and the prosecutor are using a fictitious law to convict your mother."

Once again she looked around and, not seeing anyone, continued, "I can't believe that the court would give too harsh a sentence. I think that they would want to scare you and your mother, and then they'll let you go. And now, when the judge and the rest return, listen carefully to the judge's first words. If he begins his verdict with 'the court studied this case and . . . ,' that means there will be no punishment. But if his first words are 'In the name of the law . . . ,' then know, Sasha, the sentence will be harsh, and they may take you away right from the courthouse."

Again Lyuba hugged me tight and whispered to my ear, "Sasha, dear, don't be afraid! We will pray for you very hard. I promise you that!" Tears rolling down her cheeks, she forced a smile.

As I entered the courtroom, there was hardly anyone there. My mother still sat alone in her elevated seat between two guards. I wanted so very much to call out to her, to see her face, to wave to her the way I did when I came home from school. But I understood that such a simple gesture was out of place here. Taking my seat, I just waited for whatever would happen next.

The bell sounded, and the people began to file in and take their seats. When I looked around, I could not see Lyuba. As the hall filled up, I tried again to spot her, but still could not find her. Apparently the guards had not allowed her inside the courtroom after the recess. Most likely she was just outside the door crying or perhaps praying for a favorable verdict.

The door behind the bench swung open to the same command, "All Rise! The Court is in session!" The court officials took their seats. Deep silence filled the hall. In my head I could distinctly hear the knocking of tiny hammers keeping pace with my heartbeat. Waves of heat and cold flashed through my whole body, and I felt my legs and then my whole body begin to tremble. Somewhere in my subconscious mind I understood that the judge's first words would decide my fate.

The judge took out a long page from his folder and began to

read, "In the name of this court . . ." Instantly the thought flashed through my mind, *Something very terrible awaits me*. The judge continued, "Ponomarov, Nina, from this day on is deprived of her maternal rights to her son. Her son Sasha has now become the ward of the court and will be raised in accordance with the spirit of communist ideals in a special children's home for boys." I could not hear anything else.

Sitting there, right behind the bench of the accused, waiting for the verdict, I had still hoped for a favorable outcome. But during this entire period of reprisal and repression in my country not one person accused by the authorities had ever been acquitted or had escaped punishment. Everything that had occurred here today had been preplanned in advance by the KGB.

Then my mother's voice broke through my thoughts. "Honorable Judge, I ask you, I beg you, please allow my son Sasha to spend at least three days with me. Only three days . . . please! I beg of you!" Her voice trembled.

Again total silence fell over the courtroom. Everybody waited for his reply. But instead of the judge, the prosecutor rose and began to casually collect his papers from the table and put them into the folder. Not even looking at her, he said, "We are not allowed to let your son go home. He will be taken into custody immediately and sent away to where he will continue his life."

The judge remained seated in his place and, staring into Mother's face, nervously drummed on the table with his fingers. I was convinced that he did recognize the woman who only two years before had with tears in her eyes asked him to release the driver who had run me down with his car. It seemed to me that he understood the whole dirty game in which he had to play his part. And a battle seemed to rage in his mind.

Finally he produced a piece of paper, and handing it to Mother, said, "All right, I will grant you that much, but only on one condition, that you sign this paper promising that you will not hide your son."

With trembling hand and glistening eyes she signed the document that allowed her to keep her son for three more days.

CHAPTER 9

JUVENILE JAIL

WHEN WE ARRIVED HOME, my stepfather waited in the doorway. "Why did they let you go?" he demanded. I kept quiet, not knowing how to answer him.

"How is it that you know the court's decision?" Mother countered. "After all, you weren't in court, even though, as a father, you should have been there. . . . Perhaps they have resolved all their problems and I was acquitted . . . ?"

My stepfather, still standing in the middle of the room and staring at me in bewilderment, continued, as if a new thought had struck him, "These dogs won't leave you alone until they tear you apart." Apparently he was referring to the KGB.

My stepbrother and stepsister were equally surprised to see me back home. But when they realized that I had merely a three-day reprieve, they shook their heads and mumbled, "What are you asking for, Sasha? What are you trying to prove . . . ?"

I don't remember whether I felt like crying at the time, or whether I was in a state of despair. Somehow I felt as if I had to get ready for a long journey and mustn't forget anything. Although I can't explain the feelings, it seemed as if everything had already been decreed, and all that remained for me to do was to be ready for any eventuality.

It is possible that the stories of the old Christian woman, Yelena Heideschar, had helped me to awaken from the fantasy that communism had lulled our society into. We believed and repeated the popular slogans that our country was the richest and our life the happiest of all the people in the world. The year was 1964, during Khrushchev's era. Our country, by leaps and bounds, had moved ahead in space exploration and we built gigantic factories. On holiday parades the Communist leaders displayed impressive military technology.

Most of the Soviet people were ecstatic when they saw our country's might. Everywhere we looked—on factory smokestacks, on the walls of the tallest buildings, and even in store windows—we saw huge posters with such slogans as "Glory to the Soviet People!" "Glory to the Communist Party!" "Glory to the Superior Soviet Science!" It hardly ever occurred to anybody to stop and think about the incongruity of it all. Why, for example, did we have to wait in queues by the hours for a loaf of bread. And even then not always could we get that dark loaf, often mixed with peas, corn, and some other mysterious additives? And, oh yes, the white bread. Only the sick could purchase that, and only with a special permit from a physician.

Why, in order to buy the allotted ration (four pounds) of macaroni, did we have to reserve a spot in line in the evening, and then have other members of the family take turns keeping that spot in line until the next day? And even then, we were lucky if the store's supply of macaroni lasted until we reached the counter. We had to endure similar ordeals to obtain a couple of pounds of rice, grain, or some other commodity.

The situation with dairy products was not any better, if not worse. No one knew what the Kremlin Communist leaders in Moscow thought about the millions of mothers who needed to feed their infants when milk was unavailable in stores. People regarded even half-spoiled meat or fish as a luxury, allowing it for themselves only on special occasions. We spent a good portion of our lives standing in lines.

On the other hand, vodka was available everywhere without any restrictions. And in order to forget the unsolvable problems of everyday life, many drank. No wonder Russia had become a country of drunks and alcoholics.

Life was in full swing, or as they say in Russia, "On full boil." And in the Communist "pot" they cooked up ever new promises for a happy life in the future. Although they all had a pleasant smell, the actual sampling of this ideological pot was always at least 20 years away.

To keep life from seeming dull, the Communists kept devising ever new goals and objectives, then put pressure on the poor masses to fulfill them. Often people worked two shifts in a row to build that factory before the set deadline. And when the factory was completed, the leaders rewarded the workers with medals or plaques, forgetting that the workers' families had no money to purchase clothing or meet life's most basic needs.

The first, second, and the last days of my freedom passed. The following day the police were supposed to take me into custody. But to our surprise, the fourth day came and went in peace, the fifth followed, and so the whole week flew by, and no one showed up.

Although I did not mention it to anyone, I even began to entertain the notion that Lyuba's "prophecy" had come true, that they had only intended to frighten us and everything would eventually settle down. Maybe the judge had changed his mind and allowed me to remain at home. Or perhaps those who had to carry out the court's order were so busy with other more important things, that they had no time to waste on me and had completely forgotten my existence.

With such "maybe's" in mind I went to bed each night and awakened in the morning. Each additional day of freedom seemed like yet another present to me! Just as before, I continued to attend school. Life flowed in its usual pattern, and we began to feel more and more at ease.

During the middle of the following week Mother went to a neighboring village for some provisions. Several Adventist families of Estonian extraction lived there. Stalin had ordered them exiled from their Estonian Republic, and the government had continued to refuse to allow them to return home. Knowing that our family was in dire straits, the believers of this village for a nominal price sold Mother milk, sour cream, cottage cheese, eggs, and even some flour. The food supplies usually lasted us for a whole week.

Mother usually returned from the village late in the evening. My stepfather, as always, was at work. So on that fateful day we children were the only ones at home. The entire morning we spent in school. But in the afternoon by sheer accident I saw a police car slowly pass by our house. A sudden thought paralyzed me. *They're after me . . .*

Racing outside, I dashed behind the building, desperately looking around for a safe place to hide. Too scared to stay in my own backyard, I flew over the neighbor's fence and hid there. Then through a crack in the fence I saw the police car turn around and drive off. With a sigh of relief I returned home.

My stepbrother Ivan was not at home, and my stepsister Valya sent me to the store for some salt. Just as I stepped outside the gate, I saw the police car reappear. The vehicle parked about five houses away from ours in front of the home of a notorious hooligan. It was a common sight to see a police car in front of that house. I began to reassure myself that they were not after me. They had come after our hoodlum neighbor. He must have robbed someone again.

On the way to the store I passed the car on the opposite side of the street. To my surprise I saw someone sitting in it that looked just like my stepbrother Ivan. The windows of the car were rolled up, but I still could see two or three policemen with him. They were so involved in their conversation that they didn't notice me.

Is it possible I saw Ivan in that car? I wondered. *Could he be secretly working with them?*

The line for the salt was not long, and in about an hour I was on my way home. The thought constantly churned in my head that perhaps they had come for me after all and possibly were just waiting for me to arrive home. I decided to take another route so that I would approach the house from the opposite direction. As I did, fear gripped me when I saw the police car in front of our house.

Not losing any time, I turned around and went to see one of my school friends, spending nearly an hour and a half at his house. But as I again approached my home, I saw the police vehicle still there. Thinking it best to take another long walk, I did not return until the car had left.

"Sasha, the police came for you," Valya said first thing. "They're still looking for you. Just now Ivan is with them to show them the store where I sent you."

"Is it possible that he agreed to help them arrest me?" I asked incredulously. She shrugged awkwardly and hung her head.

We were still talking as Ivan ran into the house out of breath. "They . . . the police, in the street, in the car. . . . They're asking if you're home. What shall I tell them?" he gasped.

Valya looked at me and then at the door. I could tell she wanted to help me somehow. "We could try to hide Sasha under the bed, or in the closet, and just tell them that he is not at home," she suggested.

I was ready to climb under the bed, but Ivan stopped me. "Suppose they find you? I'm scared to lie to them. We all would be in trouble then." He went outside to tell them that I was home.

Within a minute three big policemen walked into the house. "Get ready, Sasha, we came after you," they announced. I tried to explain that my parents were not home, and without their permission I never left the house.

One of the policemen produced a pair of handcuffs and, clicking them right in front of my nose, said with irritation, "We're not going to play games with you, young man. Already we have wasted plenty of time waiting for you. If we need to we'll handcuff you and toss you into the car like a stray puppy. Is that clear, kid?"

My frightened stepbrother and stepsister went into the kitchen and hid like two scared mice. In the meantime another policeman began to talk to me. "Sasha, don't be afraid of us. We'll take you to our supervisor for a short talk and then we'll bring you back home . . ." The policeman's almost square face, with a wide protruding duck-like nose and tiny worm-like lips, spread into a benign grin.

The second I agreed to go another thought began to pulsate in my head. *Don't you believe them—they're all liars.* The policeman with the manacles took my coat off the hook and ordered, "Put it on. Quickly!"

I stared at them. Dressed in their multicolored uniforms with red epaulets on their blue coats, red buttonholes, red stripes on their hats, and a lot of yellow metal buttons, they reminded me of multicolored parrots—perhaps because they, like parrots, were repeating someone else's commands.

The third policeman who had stood all this time by the door without saying a word, suddenly came to life. Grabbing me behind the back, he lifted me from the chair, took the coat from the other policeman, and forcibly began to pull it over me. Someone watching the incident might have found it somewhat ludicrous, or even perhaps sad, but I really did try to resist.

Finally the three men managed to get the coat on me, then twisted my arms behind my back and dragged me toward the car. Just before we left the house they strictly warned me not to get "smart" with them by screaming or causing a commotion. In those days the KGB always made their arrests secretly. Quietly and without arousing suspicion they abducted hundreds of thousands of innocent people, transporting them to labor camps or into Siberian exile in the far east. And just as covertly they shot them there. Many citizens did not even suspect that such monstrous reprisals took place against their next door neighbors.

The policemen literally tossed me into the car like a stray dog and took me to an unknown part of town. I remember they brought me to some large gray building. There many people in military uniforms hustled in all directions. First they led me into a spacious office in which some officious looking person in police uniform sat behind a long table. When he saw me, he giggled strangely and, waving to those who brought me in, said, "You did a fine job, you are dismissed."

When we were alone, the officer pointed to a chair and said drily, "Sit down." I carefully perched on the edge of the chair and began to study his epaulets, trying to determine his rank. Once my friends and I had studied the meaning of all the military insignias. The police insignias were quite similar to them. Now that research came in handy. Without any difficulty I ascertained that he was a colonel on the police force. Both in military and in police terms his classification was considered to be a high-level position.

The colonel leaned back in his armchair and, stroking his mustache, began carefully to scrutinize me. His face reminded me of Stalin. The same slightly curly dark hair, bushy brows, same shape mustache, and the same sly smile. Producing his pipe, he filled it with tobacco, lit it, and slowly began to talk to me. "I hope you realize where you ended up? At first it might appear somewhat frightening to you, but you will soon get used to all sorts of changes in your life. To begin with, you must forget once and for all about your parents and your home."

Tears began to flow freely. The colonel suddenly rose to his feet, approached me, and put his foot on the edge of my chair. Then he squeezed my chin with his huge fingers, pulled my face close to his, looked straight into my eyes, and hissed like a snake, "Stop sniffling. This is not a kindergarten or your church, where everyone sweetly smiles at you. Now you'll get to see another side of life. Tears won't help you here."

Letting go of my chin, he paced the room, then sat on the edge of the table. "You are now an enemy of the Soviet people. The court confirmed it. No one will ever know of your whereabouts and what your fate might be. We have done away with a lot of our enemies, and we'll continue the process until we have eliminated the last one."

As he spoke the colonel got so excited that he even pulled his revolver out of its holster. I sat motionless, just barely breathing.

Stroking his gun, the police officer looked at me as a hunter does a tiny quail, neither wanting to let it slip by, nor having the heart for the kill. Suddenly he burst out in loud laughter, approached me again, and still laughing, asked me, "Got really scared, didn't you?" My tongue stuck to the roof of my mouth, and I could barely open it, let alone speak.

Gratified by his show of force, he pushed a button on the panel of his desk. The door opened, and two police officers walked in.

The men were not the same individuals that had brought me in. "Get him out of here!" the colonel snapped.

They took me outside. At the entrance stood a police car with metal bars in the windows. My people referred to that kind of vehicle as the "Black Raven." "Put your hands behind you!" they ordered. After I did so, one of them said, "Get into the car!" The "Black Raven" had two compartments. The forward section was rather small, while the rear compartment was more like a metal cage with an iron door on it. The police officers remained in the forward compartment after they shoved me into the cage and locked the door.

Right away I clung to one of the grilled windows, but they were frosted, and I could not see where they were taking me. In about an hour the car finally stopped. The iron door opened with a rattle, and a bored voice instructed me to come out with my hands behind my back again. As I climbed out of the van I looked around, trying to figure out where I was. One policeman walked in front of me, the other followed behind. The one in back poked me with his fist and gruffly snapped, "What are you gawking around for?"

We walked through massive gates that had a sign over them announcing the place as a "Youth Allocation Center." Finding myself inside some kind of a yard, I noticed a very old and long two-story building with barred windows. Beside it were several one-story smaller structures. An extremely tall fence with barbed wire from the ground to the very top surrounded the whole cluster of buildings.

The yard was empty. Only the several old buildings with curls of paint peeling from neglect gloomily looked at me with their little narrow windows. We entered the two-story building and went to the second floor. Through one barred door I saw several teen-age boys with shaved heads. They waved at me and made some gestures, as if trying to show me something, but I could not understand them.

The police officer following behind me shoved me into some room and barked, "Sit down!" Right in front of me was a desk, behind which sat a middle-aged woman in black uniform with white metal buttons. Her features were severe—large gray eyes framed by thin eye-brows, slightly turned-up nose, thin, almost invisible, lips, and tightly pulled back snow-white hair. I sensed it would be dangerous to cross her.

Coming around the desk, she began to turn my pockets inside out and threw all the contents on the floor. In one of my pockets was a blank piece of paper and a pencil that Mother had given me just in case I needed to write her a short note. The other pocket had one ruble that I always kept for an emergency as well as a plectrum that I used to play the guitar or mandolin. She and the men took a record of every piece of clothing. After the search they put my coat and my hat inside a metal locker and locked it. Then the two police officers, after signing some papers, left the room without saying another word to me.

The woman in the black uniform examined me for a few seconds with an intense look and then asked, "What's your name?"

I swallowed and said, "Sasha."

"My name is Anna Ivanovna. From now on, Sasha, I am in charge. I will be your instructor. From the very start you ought to remember one thing: without my permission you are not allowed to do anything. And should you be disobedient, we have strict methods of corporal punishment." Continuing to study me, Ivanovna demanded, "Do you have any questions?"

Almost in a whisper, I asked, "When can my mother come to see me?"

Instantly she exploded, snapping, "Forget your parents and your home once and for all. Your mother no longer exists for you, and I don't think you will ever see her again. Perhaps when you become of age, you will be permitted to meet her again."

Her words sliced through my heart. Once more what Yelena Heideschar had said surfaced in my memory: "Whatever you are most afraid of, that will inevitably come to pass."

After a short pause, I heard Ivanovna's sharp, dry voice again. "I hope now everything is clear to you? If you have any more questions, you can come to me. And now you may join the other children."

Another woman entered and, showing me the door, said,

"You were told to go. Why don't you do as you are told? Get up and go!" I stood and walked out into the hallway. The woman accompanying me looked about 40 and was slightly plump with a big light-brown braid around her head. Her rosy cheeks, a rounded chin, and large eyes gave her the outward appearance of a kind person.

Suddenly she touched my arm and said softly, "Don't be afraid, child." A few paces further she spoke again. "My name is Maria Petrovna, but the children simply call me Aunt Masha. You too may call me Aunt Masha. And what is your name?"

My tongue became unglued, and without any difficulty I gave her my name. I even asked her if I could go to her with my questions.

Nodding her head encouragingly, she said, "Of course, of course. You can come to me any time."

To me her words were small sparks of hope.

Aunt Masha took me into a small hall containing a number of teenagers. It was a strange sight. Their heads were shaved, and they all wore the same gray clothes made of thick material. At first they all looked alike to me.

There was a chair at the entrance. I sat on it and began to observe my surroundings. The room had several tables. The boys sat around them, some playing checkers, others dominoes. Still others sat on the floor, talking softly and playing their own games. Since all were doing their own thing and talking at the same time, the place was noisy.

The room had hardly any furniture except for the worn-out tables and just as ancient-looking chairs. On the front wall, right in the center, hung a huge portrait of a smiling Lenin. Below, across the whole wall in red letters, were the words: "Thanks to Our Grand Communist Party for Our Happy Childhood!"

The left wall had two or three rows of Lenin's photographs, beginning with his childhood up to his death. It was in vogue then for every Soviet citizen to know Lenin's biography. From early childhood the propaganda authorities attempted to instill love and respect toward the founder of the Communist Party.

On the right wall, also arranged in rows, hung the flags and emblems of all the Soviet republics. Underneath the flags large letters declared: "Only in Our Highly Developed Socialist Society Can People of Various Nationalities Live as One Happy Family."

Two boys approached me, each appearing about 15 years of age. One of them was skinny and tall, the other comparatively short and stocky. Even though their heads were shaven, I could still tell that the tall boy had blond hair. He also had sky-blue eyes and was quite handsome. The other fellow, the shorter one, had a face completely covered with freckles, especially around his turned-up nose. And his hair and brows were so red, they looked as though they were dyed orange.

The tall fellow was the first to offer me his hand with the words, "Greetings. What's your name?" When I told him, he grinned sourly and asked, "What fancy job did you try to pull off that got you in here?"

At first his question sounded strange, but then I remembered that I was in a prison. Still it wasn't easy for me to explain why I was there.

"His parents are sectarians and have abused him, and that's the reason the court decided to place him under our care," Anna Ivanovna, who had followed me into the room, now interjected. "Is that clear?"

When the woman stepped aside, I told my new acquaintances, "That's not true, she is lying. I'll tell you all about it . . ."

But their faces displayed indifference, and I felt that at the moment anything I said would have been wasted on them. In turn I asked them their names.

The blond fellow called himself Sergei, and the shorter one, who to this point had only studied me and had not uttered a single word, said his name was Tolya.

Sergei bent over slightly and whispered right into my ear, "Did they manhandle you good?" Because it was their gang jargon, I could not quite understand what he wanted to know. Then he explained, "Did they search you thoroughly? Did they go through your pockets and clothing?"

Realizing that I still stared at them with a puzzled look, Tolya asked me directly, "Do you have any cigarettes on you?

We're dying for some smoke. Do you understand now?"

I shook my head and told them that I did not smoke. "You don't smoke?" they asked me in disbelief. "Then there's no point in talking with you." And they walked away.

Suddenly I heard a command, "Everybody, get in line for the toilet!" Only now did I notice that there were no girls in the hall. Standing in line behind Sergei, I asked him, "Why are there no girls here?"

He give me a puzzled look and said, "What's with you? Did you just fall off the moon? This is a juvenile prison. Prisons keep the men separately from women. Get it?" He gave me a smirk and added with a sneer, "You want girls, huh? Well, you can forget all about girls here."

Later I asked Sergei about the meaning of the sign "Juvenile Allocation Center" that I had seen at the entrance. He again smiled with a smirk and said, "Sasha, you act like a 5-year-old kid. 'Juvenile Allocation Center' is a place where they bring all the newly apprehended criminals and hold them here until they find a permanent prison placement for them."

"Then it means this is not really a prison?" I tried to be more precise.

With some irritation in his voice he answered, "This is also a prison, only it's a temporary one. Don't you get it?"

The toilet happened to be outdoors. Every two hours the prison staff took everyone outside enmass. Even though it was extremely cold, no one received either a coat or a hat. When we returned to the dayroom, Sergei came up to me with a smile that said "I know something you don't," and asked, "Hey, are you really in need of a girl?" At first I didn't get the real meaning of his question. Noticing it, Sergei began to draw me a verbal picture. "Since you asked if there were any girls around here, I figured you needed something. Even inside a prison a fellow must have some fun. So remember kid, whenever you get the urge, just tell me, and we will get you the help you need."

His eyes sparkled strangely. Patting me on the back again, he asked, "So how about those urges?" Once again I could not figure out what he was hinting at, what he really wanted from me. My inhibited behavior seemed to egg him on, and with a strange excitement in his voice, he asked bluntly, "Have you ever tried it with a girl or a woman?"

Confused, I shrugged my shoulders, and before I could say a word he grabbed me by the hand and continued in a whisper, "If you are still a virgin and haven't been kissed, then we will have to initiate you in this noble art, I am sure. Once you try it, you'll like it.

"Now listen to what I am going to tell you. In this prison works a young woman with whom many of our fellows have a lot of fun at night. I think you will find it very interesting not only to watch, but then to try it for yourself. Right now I am not sure what night she will be on duty. But we will find out and let you know in plenty of time. After all, I think it is time for you to enter adult life."

I continued to stare at Sergei with bewildered, even scared eyes. But he, caught up in his excitement, continued, "You have probably noticed that all women teachers here in prison smoke, yet they forbid us to smoke. Just about all do sex with prison guards during their night shifts. Where do you think they go off to when they lock the doors to our sleeping quarters? According to rules, they are supposed to keep watch on us. But at night there are no supervisors here, so they celebrate.

"I can see, Sasha, what I'm telling you is new to you. But, hey, once you try it, you'll like it so much we won't be able to pull you off by your ears. We'll get you some drugs and cigarettes and another world of fun will open up to you. But all in good time, not all at once . . ."

Then again whispering right into my ear he said, "No one is to know about this conversation, you understand?" Patting me on the shoulder once more, he winked at me and rejoined his buddies. And I, flabbergasted by all that I had heard, just sat there as though nailed to the chair.

About an hour later a tall imposing man, accompanied by two police officers, walked into the dayroom where we were. He was a professor from the local educational institute. Everyone was told to stop whatever they were doing and pay attention to his lecture. For about 20 minutes he talked about the rules of proper social behavior: that when meeting older people, children should always greet them. That it is essential not to forget to say thanks for the food in the dining room and not to use bad language, etc.

Even though everything he said sounded quite persuasive, and at times even interesting, no one paid any attention to him. Many youngsters yawned loudly, looked out the windows, and whispered among themselves. Then the professor began to ask questions. Unexpectedly he pointed to the redheaded Tolya and demanded, "You, for example, what are you here for?"

Glaring at the man, the redhead replied in a hoarse voice, "That, of course, is none of your business. But since you asked, I'll tell you why: I was robbing people in trains. I just happened to be careless one time, and they caught me."

The tone of his voice dripped with such sarcasm and contempt that even one of the police officers jumped up from his place and yelled at Tolya, "How dare you, punk, speak like that to the professor. You talk like that again, and I'll make mincemeat of you!"

The redhead calmly looked at the police officer and, smiling venomously, said, "You, comrade police, are behaving very rudely. Just now the professor taught us how to be courteous, and you obviously did not pay any attention. Now you ruined the whole lesson. You yell at me as though I stuck a knife in your back, but I haven't done anything bad to you yet."

The guard, after again threatening the kid with his fist, sat down and kept quiet. The professor, continuing to act like a kind uncle, again began to speak beautiful but unrealistic phrases about the wonderful life under Communism.

After supper I walked into a room that had a window that looked out into the street. Although it was getting dark, I saw people bustling in different directions. There, on the other side of the barred windows, life went on as usual. The houses and the part of the street that I could see seemed familiar to me. I clung to the window even closer and began to study the surrounding area. Yes, it was the bus stop where Mother and I transferred on the way to church.

Involuntarily I began to cry quietly and to talk to myself. "Is it really true I cannot see my Mother ever again? Is it true I can never again attend a worship service and meet the kind believers from our church? Does that mean I'll have to spend the rest of my life here?" As never before I wanted to feel free again, to have people stop shouting at me or ordering me around. I stood there and just let the tears flow, while the twilight outside kept getting thicker and thicker until it became completely dark.

Suddenly I heard a sharp, rough voice behind me. "What are you doing here?" Turning around, I saw Anna Ivanovna. In her hands she held a rubber club, and staring fiercely at me, she said, "I've been looking for you all over the place, and here you are, standing in another room without my permission. Remember, I warned you that you are not to do anything without permission? We just got through punishing one punk for disobedience. I am sure he won't forget that beating for days to come. Looks like you want to be next . . ."

Towering over me, she shook the club in the air. I stared around in terror, searching for a place to hide. But realizing that I could not escape, I began to plead for forgiveness for going into a room without permission. Seeing my tear-smeared face, my horror-filled eyes, and hearing my pitiful plea for forgiveness, she lowered her weapon and sternly said, "This time I will let you off. But I'm warning you, next time you'll be punished mercilessly for the smallest offense. And now get yourself into the day room with the rest of the group where you belong. You are not to separate yourself from the others; you must adapt to life here."

At 10:00 the staff ordered us to line up again. Anna Ivanovna opened a huge red book and began reading the names of all present. Everyone referred to the roll call as "the evening inspection." When she was sure that no one was absent, she said, "And now everyone is allowed to go to bed."

All the juveniles shared the same sleeping quarters. They showed me my bed, which happened to be next to Tolya's and Sergei's. When everybody had bedded down and everything became quiet, Sergei raised his head and asked,

"Tell us the truth, why did they bring you here? I believe you did not steal or act rowdy." Raising my head, I fixed the pillow a bit higher and began to tell them my story.

It surprised me to see their interest in what I had to say. Because I spoke in a semi-whisper those who could not hear me well sat on the beds next to mine and listened to me with rapt attention. I started by first explaining who Christians were—what we believed in and why. I told them about the Bible and the fact that Jesus had foretold that His followers at times would be hated, persecuted, and even killed. Now I had to recall as much as I could of what I had heard in sermons at worship services and what Mother had told me.

We didn't realize how quickly an hour or more passed, but their attention did not wane for one moment. And when I finished my explanation, they bombarded me with questions: "In what year will Christ come to earth the second time?" "If I don't believe in God, does that mean I'll burn up in fire?" "Can God forgive those who rob and kill people?"

Again I felt surprised at how seriously these boys responded to my answers. It seemed that they wanted to find answers to questions that had apparently troubled them for a long time. While I was sharing my faith and my story, the guard entered the room several times, but seeing that all were quietly listening and not making any noise, wandered away.

Finally everyone went to their beds, and total silence filled the room. Unable to fall asleep, I kept seeing my mother's face. I had no doubt that at that very moment she too could not sleep and thought about me. But she had no idea where I was and what was happening to me. Perhaps at that moment everyone in my family was sleeping, and she was alone on her knees fervently praying for me.

Softly I began to talk to her, telling her in my mind everything that had happened that terrible day. Thus I lay awake about an hour and a half. All around me I could hear soft puffing and snoring, but I could not fall asleep.

Suddenly I saw the redhead get up from his bed. He called Sergei in a whisper and then someone else, and they all huddled together right next to my bed and began to formulate some secret plan. Quietly I listened to their conversation. "Tomorrow night we must make our break from here," Tolya whispered. Then he gave each of the others his assignment for the breakout. Someone had to secretly check out the operation of the locks on the doors and windows on the lower floor. Another had to find out exactly who would be on duty the following night.

I heard another voice say, "I think tomorrow night Aunt Masha will be on duty. She's a simple woman. I'll try to frighten her, and if she won't behave, then I'll have to use my trusty knife on her. I got it hidden in a secret place. Leave it to me, she won't be a problem."

Everything that I heard frightened me terribly, especially the way they casually talked about murdering the only kind woman I had met there. I was afraid to move, lest I give myself away. After discussing among themselves for another hour or so, they returned to their beds. Now I could not sleep for sure. A thought seared my mind: *I have to escape too, but before they do.* Now I was preoccupied with an escape plan of my own.

Somehow I had to get permission to go to the toilet alone and, while outside, to slip through the gate and beyond the prison walls. I remembered noticing when they escorted us to the toilet that the iron gates were bolted from the inside and that the main gate had no guards. The prison had been designated for juveniles, and the authorities took it for granted that no one would dare to leave. However, the distance from the door of our building to the main gate was considerable, and to reach it could be dangerous.

Immersed in my own escape plan, I finally fell asleep.

The following morning went by according to strict prison regimen. That day I saw one boy mercilessly beaten with the rubber club for breaking some prison rule. Afterward he lay on the floor, groaning in pain, unable to rise. The prison authorities inflicted punishment in the presence of all the inmates to frighten them into submission. During my short stay in that juvenile jail I noticed a constant mutual hatred between the staff and the young convicts.

For lunch they gave us meat soup. I had no way of knowing

if the meat in the soup was beef, pork, or something else, so to be on the safe side, I offered to exchange my soup for my neighbor's rice. He gladly agreed, thinking he got the better part of the deal. I knew I had to be in good shape to escape.

After lunch the prison staff ordered us to sit through a reading session. While the instructor read, I mentally rehearsed my escape plan. Having waited for about half an hour, I raised my hand and asked permission to go to the toilet. "Be patient, you'll go together with the others," an official said curtly.

About 10 more minutes later I raised my hand again and repeated my urgent request. Involved in her story, the instructor gave me an exasperated look and mechanically said, "All right, go, but be quick about it." Since I was sitting practically in the doorway, I quietly sneaked out into the corridor, and from there, outside into the yard. It was the time when the prison workers ended their shift and were getting ready to go home. Fortunately no one was around. Peering around the corner of the building, I could see the gate about 50 paces away. But anyone observing me from the window could have instantly foiled my plan. That would have meant that I would have lost all chance of ever seeing my home again, and because of my attempt to escape, I would automatically face cruel punishment.

Even though my whole body shivered from fright and tension, I clearly understood that I could not spare a single second. Since fate had presented me with a seemingly perfect opportunity—nobody was around and the gates were only latched—I had better run now.

Dashing for the gate, with one jerk I slid the bolt to one side, and with both hands proceeded to pry the massive gate open a crack. The huge door moved a bit, and I squeezed through. I was free.

Instantly I looked around and, not seeing anyone, raced toward a five-story building and hid in its entrance. Barely catching my breath, I got my bearings and, without losing a moment, ran along the street, turning one corner then another and continuing along the next street.

The place was familiar to me, and I had already decided

which way to go. My home was about 10 miles away, and I knew that without a coat and hat in the 30 degree below zero weather I could not make it. But Mother and I passed through this area by streetcar several times on the way to visit Constantin, the associate pastor of our church. I figured his house was about three miles from where I was. I had no other choice but to run along the streetcar tracks to the last stop. From there I knew the way to his home.

At first I did not feel the cold. Only one thought dominated my thoughts—*Run! Run! Run faster!* When I realized that I had covered a considerable distance from the prison, I felt I needed to be more cautious, since all the people around me were bundled in heavy clothing, and I wore only a shirt and thin pants. If I noticed someone watching me, I slowed down and pretended I was merely going to the next house. From that house I would run to another, and from there to still another.

Somewhere behind me I heard the piercing sound of a police car siren. Instantly everything snapped. My legs buckled under me, and I felt that any minute I would collapse. Beginning to choke, I felt as if iron claws were squeezing my heart harder and harder. I just knew that it would be the end of my freedom. In my head thundered *You're caught . . . They got you . . . No use to run . . .*

Frantically I looked for a crossroad where I could turn. But the street stretched on without any turns or corners, and there was no place for me to hide. The sound of the siren grew louder and caught up with me. Without looking back I simply started to walk, expecting, any minute, someone to grab me by the shoulders, twist my arms behind my back, and drag me into the vehicle. As the car passed by me I almost stopped walking. It sped on down the road.

For a few seconds I could not comprehend what had happened. *What¿ They were not actually after me . . . ¿ This means I can still keep going . . . ¿* Some power pushed me ahead, and my feet went to work again, resuming my flight. My mind began to wrestle with what had taken place during the past couple minutes, when I was ready to surrender to the police. At the same time I began to feel the cold spreading more and more through my whole body. Just ahead I saw a five-story apartment building with several entrances. I ran into one of them to catch my breath and hide from the penetrating cold. However, when my frozen ears felt the comparative warmth of the shelter, they began to burn so much that I could not stand the pain.

Here was the final streetcar stop and the street that lead to Constantin's home. Unable to run any further, I could feel the freezing numbness in all my joints. Somehow overcoming the paralysis, I continued to walk. When I tried to slap my arms, I could not feel them. Every step was getting more and more difficult to take. Although I now saw Constantin's house, I could not go any further.

I stopped, leaned against a fence, and felt a bit warmer—and extremely sleepy. My whole body felt heavy. I wanted to sit down right there in the snow and take a short nap before continuing my journey. Then suddenly I felt as if someone had doused me with hot water. Opening my eyes, I sensed someone's presence and looked around. On the other side of the street a person was watching me. Without a doubt my strange behavior would have caught anyone's attention.

Somehow my mind continued to function, telling me that I was close to my goal and I had to move on. But my body did not want to respond to my brain. Again with everything that I had in me, I fought for the control of my numb legs. Finally I reached Constantin's home. But how could I open the fence gate? By this time my fingers could neither bend nor obey me. With great effort I somehow managed to overcome the gate and approach the window of Constantin's house.

Making one more extraordinary effort, I reached the window and knocked. The door opened. As if in a fog I saw Constantin's wife on the threshold. Seeing me, she raised her arms in dismay and without saying a word disappeared into the house again. In another second Constantin appeared in the doorway. He caught me with his powerful arms and carried me inside. I could not believe my eyes. Still, as if in a daze, I saw Mother, our pastor, and several members of our church.

As it turned out, the day I was abducted Mother had returned home from the village late in the evening, because she had had to wait a long time for the bus. When Ivan and Valya told her that the police had taken me away, she knew there was nothing that she could do or anywhere to go for help at that late hour. The following day she found the pastor and told him what had happened to me. He in turn contacted several trusted church members. They all decided to meet for a special prayer session in Constantin's house, to which I had decided to run, not quite knowing expressly why. And at the very moment I knocked on the window, they were just rising from the prayer. Needless to say, the timing of my arrival at that place was an unquestionable miracle.

Constantin had served in the navy in the extreme regions of the north for several years and knew how to help victims of frostbite. He was of a stocky, but solid frame. In spite of the fact that he had served as a naval officer, now, because of his religious convictions, he could no longer work in his specialty and had to do the most difficult and dirty work in order to put food on the table for his family.

His weather-beaten face had many tiny lines around his mouth and eyes. The gray at his temples and his smoothly combed-back hair gave him the appearance of a man who had been through tough times, yet in spite of it all had not lost his good nature. Quickly he removed my clothes and doused me with cold water. Then he placed me on the bed and began to briskly rub my whole body. After this he took some goose grease and applied it to my frozen ears and cheeks. He and his wife hastily brewed some herb tea that Constantin loved to serve to his friends. And now the tea came in handy as a remedy for frostbite.

A couple hours later I sat beside my happy Mother in the company of wonderful friends. They had prayed for a miracle, and now that their prayers were answered, they had to decide what to do next.

Constantin, the pastor, and some other young church members opted for sending me that very night to some other republic and hiding me there with some trusted believers. But those present that night included an old retired pastor whom people occasionally invited to advise them in difficult situations. The old pastor picked up the Bible, read several passages, and then said, "As Christians, we should not hide and evade any trying or difficult situation. Sasha has to go home, and we will continue to pray so that everything in his life will turn out well. And God will work out everything according to His will."

As it turned out, his words were decisive.

As Mother and I got ready to go, the others found someone's long overcoat, large mittens, and an oversized hat. In this unlikely attire I had to travel home on the bus through the entire city. Noticing my concern, someone said, "You look strange alright, but in this outfit you should be quite safe, Sasha, because nobody will ever recognize you."

Constantin gave me his hand as we left, and said, "Well, my friend, I really didn't want to let you go home tonight, but we have to oblige the elders. Should anything ever happen to you, remember, you have good, dependable friends who will never forget you." With this he gave me a big bear-hug and kissed me affectionately on the cheek.

During the trip back to my house I could not overcome a strange feeling. I felt that instead of going home, I was heading in a direction not to my liking.

CHAPTER 10

CAPTIVE AGAIN

MY REAPPEARANCE AT HOME was a big surprise to all members of my family. When my stepfather saw me, his mouth dropped open in amazement, and he remained speechless. The too-large clothing must have appeared ridiculous, but it was obvious that something unusual had happened.

As I put my own clothes on, my stepfather asked, "What fancy trick did you pull to end up back home?" I told him I had escaped from the prison. Now his eyes showed not only surprise but panic and fear. Unable to believe what he had heard, he demanded, "You mean you ran away from prison . . . ?" Lowering himself into the chair and looking at Mother with fear-filled eyes, he sighed, "Do you all realize what can happen to us because of your escape from prison?"

Of course, I didn't know what to expect. But when I had concocted the plan, and then actually executed it, I had only one thing on my mind: *Get out and be free.*

My stepbrother and stepsister were petrified. For the time being they acted as if they had lost their tongue. Silently they looked first at me, then at Mother, and finally at their father. When I went to bed, my stepfather came to me and began to explain further, trying to make a point. "I have read in books that in our country there are special torture chambers. Some of them so small that a person can only stand in it. And he cannot lean on anything, because sharp needles protrude from all four walls. And from the top, water drips constantly on the head. They keep a person in this position for hours until he becomes insane. Then they place him in a psychiatric hospital as a patient where they give him injections until he looses all of his faculties and becomes like a vegetable. After that they send him home, and he, having become incurable, remains a lifelong cripple, incapacitating the entire family in the process." After a short pause, apparently to scare me even more, he added, "There are other chambers where rats eat a person alive."

"It would be much better," Mother interrupted, "if you, like a father, would try to help and not scare the wits out of an already frightened child."

The following morning I awakened with the thought that any minute now the "Black Raven" would come after me, that they would beat me with those rubber clubs, and then take me to a nightmarish place where they would subject me to all the kinds of torture that my stepfather had described the previous night.

But the morning went by quietly and peacefully, and no one came after me for some reason. With each hour I kept reassuring myself that they had forgotten about me, and by sheer luck everything would be all right. I couldn't go outside, because I no longer had a coat or a hat. The disguise I had worn the evening before had worked only because it was dark.

After about three days Anna Ivanovna, the instructor from the Children's Prison, unexpectedly showed up at our house. In her hands she held my coat and my hat, and in her usual dry voice, she ordered, "Hurry up Sasha, get ready! I came to take you back to the Youth Allocation Center."

Seeing that she was alone, I felt daring and refused to go with her. Only my mother was at home, and the woman turned to her and with the same tone of voice ordered, "Do something about this attitude of your son and make him go with me, if you want to avoid the consequences."

Mother sadly looked at her and naively asked, "Tell me, do you have any children of your own?"

"No, I don't have any children," Ivanovna coldly replied. "What are you trying to imply?"

Tears sparkled in my mother's eyes as she said softly, "In that case you won't be able to understand."

Throwing my coat and hat on the floor, Ivanovna ran up to me, grabbed my shoulders, and began to shake me and shout, "I'm telling you, get ready immediately! Or I'll call the police, and they'll handcuff you and toss you into the car like a no good mongrel pup."

Tearing loose from her grip and looking her straight in the eyes with disgust, I said, "I want the police to come here right now. I want them to twist my arms and treat me like a dog and toss me into the car. I want to see and feel once again what kind of free country I live in. And I promise I will never forget what you put me through as long as I live!" Finally she understood that I would not come, and without saying a word, she flew out of the house and slammed the door with such force that the windowpanes rattled in their casings.

Another slow week passed, filled with bleak anticipation. The fact that no one came after me both tormented and comforted me at the same time. I started attending school again. There at least I could occasionally forget the constant anxiety.

The school had a new principal. The following Monday my teacher, Olga Petrovna, said that a school official wanted to see me. As I walked along the hallway, I prepared myself to meet the new principal, who, I expected, would smoke a lot, shout at me, call me all kinds of names, and threaten me.

My assumptions proved me wrong. The old principal's office, where Lenin's portrait still hung, was no longer muffled in dark drapes. Instead, the windows were open and the room appeared bright and fresh. The new principal was a tall friendly man with a pleasant smile. He seamed to speak like a friend and even offered me a chair. Then he introduced himself. "My name is Pavel Ivanovich."

It was strange that the new principal did not smoke or shout at me, but spoke in a quiet, soft voice. He asked me about my family: where they worked, if we had enough money to live on.

Cautiously I answered his questions. But to my surprise he remained calm and amiable.

It was evident from his questions that Pavel Ivanovich was interested in our church and what we believed in and why. Finally, he spoke to me in a serious but compassionate tone, "Sasha, you must understand that if you refuse to attend school on Saturdays, they will pick you up again, and neither I nor anybody else could help you. The court's decision must be carried out. And even though I feel sorry for you and your parents, I have no power to reverse the sentence." After a short pause he continued, "Today they called me from the children's prison and said that soon they'll come after you, but exactly when I don't know."

Rising, he approached me and softly urged, "Think about it, Sasha. Will you have enough patience and strength to remain true to your Christian ideals to the end? And now go to your class."

As I left the principal's office, I felt as if I had spent time with a good person who tried to extend me a helping hand, but who himself was shackled. His sympathetic tone of voice and his kind manners were welcome encouragement.

During the fourth period that same day someone knocked on the classroom door. Olga Petrovna left the classroom and talked a long time with an individual in the hallway. Naturally I nervously watched the door. *That must be the police. I'm done for.* Finally Petrovna returned and, looking at me, said, "Sasha, your mother came after you." I knew it could not be my mother. It was the police, and I had to prepare myself for the worst.

When I left the classroom and entered the hallway, I saw two police officers and the fat-lipped chekist whom I had last seen in the court. The chekist talked with the principal, and I heard him repeating to Ivanovich, "You ought to understand that the court's decision must be carried out."

Approaching one of the police officers, a tall, broad-shouldered man, I asked, "Where is my mother?"

The policeman gave me a crooked, sarcastic smile and, pointing to the exit, said, "There by the porch." Without further hesitation I dashed toward the door. Outside, right by the porch, waited a large police car. Automatically, I tossed my briefcase aside and took off.

Behind me I heard the boots of one of the men racing along the school corridor. The other man picked up the chase. Suddenly I heard a crash behind me. Quickly turning around, I saw a red militia hat bouncing down the steps of the portico, while the big militiaman lay spread-eagle on the very edge of the vestibule. It was a pretty funny sight.

Apparently he did not expect me to run, and having abruptly darted after me, forgot that outside the surface was extremely slippery. So he stumbled in one big swoop and flopped on the cement landing right in front of the steps. Although I wanted to laugh, my mind was on my desperate flight, so I ran.

Once again I could hear the same thunder of boots behind me and the man's heavy breathing. Of course while I was taking two or three strides, he needed to make only one and quickly caught up with me. Like a hawk he swooped down on me, grabbed me by the shoulders, and began to drag me toward the car. Since my overcoat was unbuttoned, I slipped out of it and resumed my flight, leaving the giant with the coat in his hands.

Instantly he caught up with me and in a wheezing voice said, "You won't get away, you pup . . . You're mine . . ." In a few more hops he had me again. This time he grabbed me by my arms and dragged me to the car.

I began to scream from pain and anger. "What are you doing to me? Just because I'm a believer, you drag me to jail? Leave me alone, I want to live with my parents! Now I see what kind of freedom we have in our country! Let me go!" The louder I screamed, the tighter he clasped my arms in his iron grip.

When he dragged me back to the car, I saw Mother waiting on the portico. She stood there and helplessly wept. Next to her stood the other policeman, restraining her.

At this moment the school bell rang, and all the students poured outside for recess. I kept resisting, while the policeman, with the help of the chekist, tried to pull me toward the car door. One of my classmates, a chipper fellow named Vovka, shouted loudly, "I wish we could record this scene on a movie camera and show it on television to the whole nation so all

could see how our militia treats the Christians in our country."
Several passersby stopped and froze in disbelief at the scene.

Wrestling me to the car door, they opened it and tried to
shove me in. But I spread my arms so they could not force me
in. Then the chekist came from behind and struck me on the
back with his fist. My arms became numb with pain. He twisted
them behind my back and with a thud flung me into the car.

I was scratched and bloody from being dragged on the
ground. When the car started moving, I opened my eyes and saw
my mother's face in front of me. "Are you alright, son?" she
asked. I nodded to indicate that I was OK.

A few minutes later, as I regained my senses, I remembered
that the incident had occurred in front of the school. I sat up and
looked around. In the front seat I saw the two policemen and the
chekist. They smoked and chatted cheerfully among themselves.
The chekist turned around and said to Mother, "Be thankful that
I took you along. But your son is pretty stupid to behave like a
fool in front of all the people." Then he looked at me like a ven-
omous snake and hissed, "So, you tried to escape? And what
was all that screaming about? Did you want to alert all the
passersby and all the students? Well, none of them helped you,
and now you're back in our hands."

Interrupting him, I said loudly so that all could hear, "You
can't hold me, I'll run away again!"

A loud laughter filled the car, and the fat-lipped chekist
threatened, "Now you won't ever escape. We'll take you to a
place from where you will never be able to find your way back."

"Let me freeze," I snapped. "Let me die on the way, but you
can be sure of one thing: I'll run away again. I'll never stay in
your prison."

"We shall see how you can manage that," the chekist replied,
a note of irritation in his voice. "And now shut up and at least
spare your mother the pain, if you have no pity for yourself."

Bringing us to the same juvenile prison, this time the authorities allowed Mother to go inside. They took us to a small room
on the second floor containing only two chairs, and told us that
we had exactly 15 minutes to ourselves. Mother embraced me

and held me close, as she used to do when I was small, and began to stroke my hair. "My dear son, you are now 12 years old," she said softly. "The same age Moses was when he parted with his mother to live in a royal place. But instead of going to live in a palace, your lot is a prison.

"I don't know why all this is happening to you, and I cannot explain it, but I am totally convinced that God will not leave you, not for one minute. Your faith is being tested Sasha, and it will become apparent whether or not you are a true Christian."

I listened to her every word. As never before, it seemed important to me to remember everything she told me. I could not even imagine when, if ever, I would see her again. No one could foresee what might happen the next day or the day after.

Mother continued stroking my head with her warm hand. "I'll always be thinking of you, and will pray for you without ceasing. I believe that God has a special plan for you, if you only live through this difficult time."

The 15 minutes flew by. The door burst open, and a man in black prison uniform announced, "Your time is up."

Tears began to stream down Mother's cheeks. She pressed me against her once more and said in a whisper, "If you have the smallest opportunity, write to me at least a few words. Tell me how you feel and where you are. I will be waiting for some message from you. Take care of yourself, darling! I will pray hard for you!"

The attendant pulled us apart and pointed to the door. Mother left, leaving me alone once again.

The door opened again. Her face distorted by a malicious grin, Anna Ivanovna entered. "So, the little sparrow got caught, did he? The time has come to settle the score for your breakout and for your rude behavior in your home when I had come for you."

Fury filled her pale-blue, washed-out eyes. And as she spoke, her ugly steel-capped front teeth added to the unpleasantness of her face. She pressed a red button by the door, and two prison workers in black uniforms burst in with the question, "What happened?"

"Nothing just now," the woman answered calmly, "but a few

days ago that worthless brat ran away from our institution. And now we must teach him a lesson so that in the future he will never again get the urge to repeat such a stupid act."

"Should we administer the punishment in the presence of others," one of the men asked, "or right here and now?" The tone of his voice clearly indicated that she was his superior, and that they were here to carry out her orders. She gave me her imperious look and commanded, "Punish him right here!"

I cannot convey to you the fear that filled me for a few seconds. The shock of it rendered me totally speechless, but my body began to tremble. They ordered me to lie on the floor. I knew that asking for mercy was pointless. Prostrating myself with my face to the floor, I shut my eyes.

They beat me with rubber rods mainly on my rear end and occasionally on my back and legs. After the first and the second blow, I felt as if my senses had somehow vanished for a few seconds. Then I began to hear their voices again. And after several more blows, complete silence replaced the roaring in my head, and everything around me somehow vanished.

I remember coming to when someone poured cold water on my face. One of the men asked, "Maybe it's enough for first time?"

"I think it will be enough for today," Ivanovna replied indifferently. "Otherwise, he might just drop dead on us."

Someone began to shake me violently on the shoulders. As I lifted my head with difficulty, one of the prison staff roughly commanded, "Get up! Enough lying around here!" I tried to get up, but my whole body burned with pain, and I collapsed on the floor again.

"Let him lie there another five minutes," Ivanovna said with the same cold indifference. "You may go now. Thanks for your help," she told the attendants. I felt as if I would not be able to get up even after five hours, let alone five minutes.

The woman again began to shake me by the shoulders. "Get up, make it quick, if you don't want me to add to your punishment." I don't remember how, but somehow I managed to get up, and, limping from the pain in my left leg, I went into the dayroom. Apparently they had hit me hard on my left leg, the one that had been broken when the car had run me down, and now it hurt terribly.

I was glad to see an empty chair in a corner by the window. But when I sat down, it felt as though I'd been sitting on a hot plate. With a moan I got to my feet. But I could not stand long either. Again, gingerly leaning against the wall, I lowered myself onto the chair and shut my eyes.

I wanted to lie down. I wanted to cry. I wanted to tell someone my pain and hurt. I felt as if I was in a dark forest surrounded by wild beasts. And to avoid angering the beasts I had to sit very quietly. At the same time I felt as if I had been left alone in a desert without a single living being around.

Half an hour or more crawled by. Even though my pain did not subside, I began to notice people and things around me. I saw many teenagers in the dayroom, who, as before, were close-shaven and dressed in gray uniforms. But I could not spot Tolya, Sergei, or any other familiar faces among them. Where were they all?

No one came up to me. Only a few watched me out of the corners of their eyes. I found it extremely hard to conform and become part of this alien society. But I understood that I had no other choice but to try to make contact with those around me.

As I looked around the room, I saw the same pictures and photographs of Lenin and the beautiful-sounding slogans on the walls. Everything remained the same. Except this time I noticed red buttons mounted into the walls around the auditorium and next to the doors. Because of my beating I knew precisely what those buttons signified. I also understood why Ivanovna was not afraid to be alone among young criminals. At any moment all she needed to do was press one of those buttons and armed aides would instantly come. She herself wore a pistol on her belt. Only now was I becoming aware of such things, but those who had been here a long time already knew the rules.

Now I noticed that I was the smallest of all the boys there. After all, I was not quite 13 yet. The rest were at least 15 years of age. Maybe the authorities had placed me here in order to intimidate me into abandoning my religious convictions.

The command, "Get in line for lunch," made me stagger from my chair. As we walked into the dining hall, one boy asked me, "What did you get in here for?" It was usually the first question people used in prison to get to know someone. I told him that I would explain later.

I still did not know all the cruel prison rules. Later I learned that every prisoner memorized all the codes and statutes of the criminal law by numbers, and which violation had brought him here. So when someone asked, "What are you here for?" one might answer, "I am here for paragraph 126," or some other regulation. Unfortunately I did not know even that much, so I could not tell anybody why I was in prison.

After lunch the aids took us to the restrooms. As we were standing in line, the same boy who had asked me why I was there came up to me. Even though his hair was black, somehow he reminded me of Tolya, the redhead. Perhaps it was the freckles covering his entire face. But then maybe it was his brazen look and his rough manners.

Staring at me with a peculiar disdain, he said, "So, sucker, I guess we don't know each other yet. Let's get acquainted. My name is Igor, but my friends—and my enemies—call me Tarzan. Now you too can call me that. I am the leader of one of the robber gangs, and I am not used to not getting answers to my questions. And now my pals will teach you some of our rules."

He turned to the boys behind him and, rubbing his hands, said, "This infant needs a lesson in manners." Even before he finished speaking, one of the boys struck me in the face. The blow knocked me against the wall, and I slowly sank to the ground. In the wild excitement of being able to attack a defenseless victim, Tarzan's cohorts kicked me in the stomach a couple more times and said, "This is in honor of our acquaintance—something for you to remember."

My whole body ached from the flogging, and now my agony increased even more. I felt something warm run down my face. When I brushed my hand across my face I noticed that it was covered with blood. They picked me up and told me to wipe the blood off my face with snow to erase the traces of their beating.

The snow on the farside of the bathroom was yellowish in color, no doubt from urine. I wanted to go around to wipe off the blood with clean snow, but they held me back and threatened, "Do you think you are going around to show your pretty face? I'm telling you for the last time, wipe your face here, or we'll have another short talk with you."

Everything around me seemed to be muffled, hazy, and distant. At times my mind would clear up and I could see my surroundings but could not comprehend anything. If my mother had seen me at that moment, her heart would have failed her.

After rubbing my face with smelly yellow snow, I then wiped it with my shirt and got back in line. I was convinced that the prison guard saw the whole scene but pretended not to notice anything.

When we returned to the dayroom, I found my chair in the corner by the window and carefully sank onto it, then rested my head in my hands and closed my eyes. Never had I been so miserable. Everything around me appeared unreal and frightening.

The prison aides had beaten me with rubber rods, and I could not turn to anyone for comfort. Clearly the only thing left for me to do was to keep my mouth shut. The prison staff watched me constantly, and the idea of escape was unthinkable. The other prisoners stared at me with contempt, because I was different and did not understand their rules or lingo. In other words, I was not one of them.

The whole world, it seemed, had turned against me. Then somehow a thought came to mind. *It's alright, Sasha. Christians in the Dark Ages had it far worse. They endured it and so will you.* So I sat there until evening, waiting impatiently for permission to go to bed. With every hour the pain increased throughout my whole body, and at times I felt that any moment now I would collapse and just die.

Because of my pain I could not eat any supper, and I continued to sit alone and softly cried so that no one could see. The hand on the clock appeared to be frozen to the face of the clock and refused to move to 10:00. But, as everything on earth comes

177

to an end, so too did that long, nightmarish day.

During the night I had a high fever and chills. With difficulty I climbed off the bed and, swaying from side to side, approached the night watchman sitting by the door of our sleeping quarters and told him that I was sick. Those on night duty were usually men, but occasionally women also were assigned. That night it was a man, someone I saw for the first time. When I told him I was sick, he gave me a skeptical look and said, "If you have a high fever, I can give you a pill, but to see the doctor, you'll have to wait until morning."

With a look of irritation he opened a small first-aid box hanging on the wall. Then giving me another distrustful look, he grumbled, "Do you at least know what kind of pill you want?" I remembered the names of the medicines Mother had given me when I had fever, then asked him for a glass of water, but he only waved with his huge hand and said, "Never mind, do without water."

All night I tossed in bed from fever and excruciating pain. It is possible that I dozed off for a few minutes, but it seemed I did not sleep the whole night. If during the day I could hardly wait for night to come, now I impatiently waited for morning, hoping to receive some kind of help.

In the morning Aunt Masha approached my bed. Feeling my head, she said compassionately, "He's burning up with fever." I was happy to see her. Her gentle words sounded like the sound of the voice of an angel. She brought me a large cup of water, found another blanket, covered me, and said, "Poor child, you got yourself into this wild crowd, and now you must suffer here with these rough-neck criminals."

Two hours later the doctor showed up. After the examination he allowed me to stay in bed the rest of the day. They left me alone all day, and only when everybody went to the dining hall, did they send one of the boys to get me.

My thoughts constantly dwelt on home. To my surprise, I kept thinking not of my neighborhood friends with whom I had loved to chase the soccer ball around the courtyard, but of my church friends with whom I now wanted to be more than ever before.

Two days later I felt considerably better, and even though my left leg still gave me a hard time, at least I could get up, limp along, and sit or move around. After breakfast Tarzan came up to me and said with a mocking grin, "How are things, hero? You probably thought you'd die from pain, but I see you survived."

I did not say anything in reply, but after a short pause he continued, "We didn't know that you had gotten 'peppered' by the 'Dogs.' [That's how they referred to the prison guards.] That is why we gave you some of our own 'training' by the restrooms the other day, but if you had told us about the rubber rod beating you got, we wouldn't have touched you. We ourselves have had a taste of the rubber rods more than once, so we know all about it."

Then he slid his chair close to me and asked again, "Now, are you going to tell me what you are here for?" I understood that my explanations should be precise without extra details.

"You see, Tarzan," I began, "I am a believer, and because I go to church and . . ."

He cut me short and covered my mouth with his hand. "Stop right now! A believer, you say? What faith do you belong to? There are lots of them now."

"I'm a Christian."

"I also believe in God and Christ—sort of," Tarzan interrupted again. "For example, when I was small I had a little accident. One day, while my parents were gone, I forgot to close the faucet in the kitchen. The sink overflowed and water flooded the floor. When I saw what had happened, I didn't know what to do. We had a wood floor, and all the boards were soaked through.

"My father was an alcoholic, and I knew for sure he would get me for letting it happen. I thought I was a goner. In my grandmother's chest there was a small icon with a picture of Jesus on it. I took it out and asked the icon to help me. I fell asleep holding the icon in my hands. When my parents returned, my father didn't say a word to me. From that day on I began to believe that some kind of God does exist, except I don't know Him. And that's why I am not totally sure that I fully believe in

Him. Sometimes I do and sometimes I doubt."

From somewhere I felt new energy and began as best I could to explain Christ and the Gospel to him. And again I was surprised that everything I told him he listened to with great interest. Even things that had seemed less than exciting to me in church now captivated the young convict.

We talked about two hours. Tarzan's eyes warmed up a bit and his usual gloomy face cheered up somewhat. I even stopped being afraid of him. In turn he was no less surprised that I could answer his questions. After almost everything I would say he would comment, "How in the world do you know all this?"

By now our conversation had taken on the appearance of a friendly relationship. "Sasha, can you write me a prayer?" Tarzan asked me at one point. Then, as Mother used to do with me, I began to explain to him that prayer is a conversation with God, and it would be better if he addressed Jesus in his own words. But Tarzan shrugged and replied in confusion, "I've never prayed in my whole life, and I've no idea where to begin or end a prayer or what to say to God."

On a small piece of paper I wrote him a simple prayer. He thanked me, and in all seriousness added, "I would like it very much if you would tell the members of my gang all that you told me. I think you still remember that I am a gang leader. In the past I pulled off quite a few dandies—when I had my freedom."

He showed me the palms of his hands and proudly declared, "Through these hands passed many thousands of rubles. True, they were stolen, and yet were 'earned' easily."

That same evening I sat in the circle of Tarzan's friends, telling them about Jesus, my church, and about what I believed in and why. And of course I gave them answers to their most startling questions. Involved with my story, I did not even notice at first what Tarzan was doing. I could not believe my eyes when I realized that he was crocheting a bright red rose on a small piece of cloth. A thief, a gang leader, and there he sat crocheting. It just did not make sense to me. Apparently, like most normal boys of his age, he had a girlfriend. And as he told me later, he had promised her that the next time they met he would give her an unusual gift.

Showing me his needle work, he explained, "I used to give her lots of money and gold rings and stuff. But even rings with rare gems wouldn't be anything out of the ordinary for her. But if I give her a symbol of my love for her, done with my own hands, that will really blow her away. I know that at first she won't believe that it is my own work. But then I'll show her how I do it."

I listened to that young outlaw and tried to understand how this rough, brutal person, who without a second thought would stab or maim just about anybody for money, could at the same time love someone so tenderly.

When I was alone, I began to think about escaping again. In a couple days, when the prison had collected a certain number of prisoners, the authorities would transport us on special trains somewhere far away to the north of the Kazakh republic. There in the depth of the taiga, the swampy forests of Siberia, waited huge prisons for adults as well as for youth offenders. The thought that I would soon end up in a large prison camp patrolled around the clock by armed guards made my heart stand still and left me feeling totally helpless. And I knew there really was nothing that I could do about it.

Yet, in spite of all this, I never stopped thinking of some way to escape. I clearly understood that my prospects here were indeed bleak. The thought of the approaching Sabbath especially filled me with dread. As a rule, it was the day they made a thorough house-cleaning throughout the whole prison. How could I refuse to work on it? Without a doubt, I would receive another beating.

As an Adventist I had almost daily problems in the dining hall. I did not know what might contain pork. Plus my Christian lifestyle would undoubtedly bring me other difficulties.

After my conversation with Tarzan, and then with his friends, their attitude toward me had drastically changed. They treated me as one of their own, explaining to me the rules of prison life. For example, they warned me that if I had any money or anything of value I had better not try to hide it, since they would find it anyway and take it away from me after beating me for not trusting them. Because they never stole from each other, they left any money in the open. According to another of their rules, if I were ever to divulge something to the "Dogs," the other inmates would beat me mercilessly. And if I ever sold out to the "Dogs," the prisoners would get even with me.

That evening I decided to speak with Tarzan and confide in him my desire to escape. Calling him aside, I whispered, "I have to tell you something very important, but no one else should hear it."

Tarzan picked up a book from the floor and motioned with his eyes to follow him to the corner of the room. "Get yourself a chair," he said, "and we'll sit here pretending we're reading a book together while we talk." Opening his book, he looked into it, then asked, "Alright, let's have it. What happened?"

For a while I could not hide my nervousness. Searching for the right words to say, I fought with indecision. The young but experienced gang-leader noticed my agitation and again insisted "What happened? You can talk freely. Don't be afraid of me. I can keep a secret, and I won't hurt you."

Stuttering I began, "You see, Tarzan, I simply must get out of here. But I am afraid if someone finds out about it, my chances will be ruined and I will never be able to escape again."

"Why would you want to run away, Sasha," he protested, "when on the outside you can't even find any bread in stores? Here at least we get plenty of white bread to eat. They don't make us work that hard or send us to school. The most important thing for us is to pass the court-appointed time and avoid as much work as possible.

"Hey, we always have plenty of cigarettes. And even if we want a woman, we know what counselor to turn to—yes, my friend, some of them are always ready and willing. Trust me, life here isn't all bad."

"Tarzan, you have to understand me," I interrupted. "I am entirely a different kind of person, and everything you mentioned does not interest me. I need your help to organize my escape from here."

Tarzan closed his eyes, and it was clear that he was seriously thinking about something. After a few seconds he gave a loud sigh and said decisively, "Listen to me very carefully—no one is to know anything about our conversation. I have noticed that for some reason, Sasha, they are watching you more than anyone else. Therefore we need to wait for the prison staff to become convinced that you are not interested in another escape."

"But if we wait a few more days, it might be forever too late. They are getting ready to take us to Siberia, and then I won't be able to get out for sure."

"Hey, take it easy!" he said, looking at me sternly. "Otherwise you yourself will ruin everything. Besides, I noticed that now they not only bolt the main gate, they also lock it. All of this happened, apparently, after your last escape and the subsequent unsuccessful breakout of another gang just before we were brought here."

Then he told me what he had heard from others. During the same night that I had made my get-away, 15 or more other teenage inmates had also attempted an escape. They had seriously wounded a night supervisor and another prison guard with a knife. But the alarm system had worked, and the armed guards had quickly caught them and transferred them to a high security prison. There they were being kept in solitary confinement, awaiting their new trial.

When he ended his sad story, Tarzan said meditatively, "To attempt an escape at night, when the alarm system is activated, is sheer nonsense."

When he told me about the failed escape attempt, I immediately thought, *How strange that I succeeded. After all it was my first try. Surely, a special power must have directed, guided, and protected me.*

Curious as to what was going on in Tarzan's mind, I asked, "You think there really is no chance for me?"

"Take it easy, Sasha," he said sternly. "It doesn't pay to take unnecessary chances, if you want to do it right. Tomorrow I will tell you exactly what we will do. Meanwhile, keep your mouth shut. Try not to arouse even the slightest suspicion."

The following day happened to be a Friday. In the morning, at the first opportunity, I asked Tarzan what he thought about the possibility of escape. But he was in a foul mood and only angrily mumbled, "Don't fidget! I haven't forgotten. When the right time comes, I'll tell you what you have to know. Act like a man and learn to wait. This is all I can tell you for now."

Not daring to risk any more questions, I only sighed heavily and walked away. My other big problem that I faced was how I was going to spend the upcoming Sabbath. On the one hand, I understood that I was not supposed to work on the Sabbath. On the other hand, I rationalized, I was in rather extreme circumstances, and God wouldn't count it against me if I, as required, along with the rest of the boys, did some prison chores.

But if I could thus justify working on the Sabbath, then what was I doing here in the first place? Why didn't I just go to school on Saturdays with the rest of them? The commandment said, "thou shalt not do any work." What did "any work" mean? Did it allow me to choose what I could and could not do?

From the time I rose in the morning—making the bed, going to breakfast, spending time with the other teens in the dayroom—I constantly reasoned with myself, trying to settle in my mind what I should do the nest day. I definitely was in a quandary. I still remember that something that I had heard once in a sermon long before particularly troubled me. "A small concession gives rise to a big vice," the speaker had said.

When "Aunt Masha" walked into the dayroom, I was glad for the opportunity to find out from her how the prison generally spent its Saturdays. Without attaching any significance to the question, she simply explained that generally all inmates had to clean up the prison quarters.

I asked her to be more specific. "What exactly are we expected to do?"

She looked at me curiously. "Why is it so important for you to know in advance? Tomorrow you can find out for yourself."

At that moment I had to overcome my timidity. "You see, Aunt Masha," I said point blank, "according to my religious beliefs, I cannot work on Saturdays. And so I'd like to ask you to give me some work today to make up for tomorrow. I'll be glad to do whatever you ask of me."

My request sounded so outrageous to her that her jaw dropped from surprise. Clearing her throat, she asked again, "What did you say about your religious beliefs?"

I repeated everything from the beginning, feeling that Aunt Masha had never heard of any such beliefs in all her life. She scrutinized me, as if trying to assure herself that I was not crazy, then weakly added, "Well, if you want to work today for tomorrow, I'll tell you what to do."

She assigned me to dust all the chairs, tables, window sills, and the beds in our sleeping quarters. My having learned housekeeping chores at home came in quite handy this time. I finished everything in no time. When I reported to her that I had finished the task, she started to find fault with my performance. But discovering that I had done the job conscientiously, she said, "You did your share of work for tomorrow."

Even though my fellow inmates made snide remarks and glances at me as I cleaned, I, for the first time there, felt quite pleased with myself. It even seemed to me that my legs and back did not hurt so much anymore, and I wanted to do additional work to earn Aunt Masha's approval. But she shook her head and said, "That's enough. You did a good job." Still I wanted to prove to everybody that I had earned my day off. So I insisted that she give me more work.

Finally she gave me a bucket of water, a huge rag, and told me to scrub the floor in our sleeping quarters. Although the job seemed much more involved than the previous one, I attacked it anyway. A couple hours later I finished crawling with a rag under the beds and in the aisles. My back and my left leg by now hurt badly, but nonetheless I was happy that tomorrow, on my Sabbath, I would not be required to do any work. I felt somehow reassured that even in such difficult circumstances I was able to observe my Sabbath according to God's commandment.

On Sabbath morning after breakfast, everyone lined up to receive his housekeeping assignment. I felt rather at ease, knowing that Anna Ivanovna had the day off and the other instructor, though strict, was not at all hostile toward me. Just then Aunt Masha walked into the hall and told the instructor, "Sasha will be under my

185

supervision today, he will be helping me today." As we left the hall, Aunt Masha suggested, "Why don't you go to the library and get yourself something to read to make your time pass faster."

The "library" consisted of four bookcases standing right in the hallway. I took a quick glance at the titles on the shelves. The books were mainly fairy tales and volumes for very young readers. One shelf was reserved for Soviet propaganda and the life of Lenin. By sheer accident, I saw among the thicker books a familiar title: *Uncle Tom's Cabin.* I had heard our pastor make some comments about the book, and other believers had spoken favorably of it, so I selected it without any hesitation.

A door opened a crack, and I saw Aunt Masha peering through it. "I see you found a good book, and now let's go over to my 'kingdom.'" She had a tiny space under a staircase leading to the second floor. It was so cramped that a small dilapidated nightstand and an ancient three-legged stool barely fit inside. Against the other wall stood several buckets and mops. And on a nail hung Aunt Masha's coat.

Sliding the stool closer to the wall, she said, "You may sit on it, it'll support you, if you won't move it from the wall. If someone knocks, be quiet and don't answer. I'll return when the general cleanup is done."

The door creaked shut, and I was alone. A feeling of special joy and thanksgiving filled my whole being. I could not get over the fact that while I was in prison God had still granted me a Sabbath's rest. Spontaneously I knelt down, and a prayer of thanksgiving to God simply poured out of me. When I had entered that prison I had never imagined that I would be spending my Sabbath this way. I had been preparing myself for the worst, but everything had turned out so well.

And the book interested me. As I read page after page, I began to empathize more and more with the Blacks living in distant America. The author depicted the White people as heartless, selling and trading the Blacks as if they were personal property. Indignation toward the cruel slave masters filled my mind. As I pondered over that book, suddenly I had the thought that my present situation greatly resembled that of the Blacks in America during that period of history.

For a time I set the book aside as I struggled with a number of questions: Why did my country abuse and deprive believers of their rights almost as much as slavery had the Blacks in America? I wasn't guilty of any crime. Why did the Soviet Union arrest Christians and imprison them? Why were the Communists so brutally mistreating us? Why did no one in our country come to the defense of thousands and thousands of innocent Christians who were tortured and even savagely murdered, as Yelena Heidescher had told me? That meant my country too had slaves and slave masters.

Again I began to read the book that had upset me so much.

The door creaked, and Aunt Masha walked in. I got up from the chair, expecting it was time for me to leave. Waving her arms, she quickly whispered, "Don't hurry. 'Polit-information' is being conducted in the dayroom. You can stay here a bit longer." "Polit-information" was a time when a prison instructor or some outside speaker would read newspaper articles and commentaries about the political situation around the world.

I flipped a bucket upside down and sat on it, and let Aunt Masha have the stool. Lowering herself onto the three-legged stool, she arranged her lavish braid. It was very becoming to her, softening her face. She looked at me with her kind, smiling eyes, and asked, "How did you spend the day? Weren't you bored?"

I told her that the day had gone quickly for me, since I was thoroughly engrossed in the book I was reading. She looked at me, sighed heavily, and said sadly, "Soon, my child, they'll take you far, far away from your native home. I've heard that they're compiling a list of prisoners for a distant prison camp on Monday or Tuesday. So get ready for a very long journey . . ."

Her statement confirmed the rumors I had heard myself about soon being transferred to a regular juvenile prison colony. Putting her hand into her bosom, she pulled out a small aluminum cross on a thin string. She looked at the cross, then at me, and in a fearful voice confided, "You see, I too am a Christian, but I'm afraid to talk about it openly; otherwise, they'll fire me for sure, and I have children and family to support.

"I attend our Orthodox church rarely, just once or twice a year, but even then after service I come home all upset. Our priests behave like atheists. They smoke, drink vodka, and even dip into sacred funds. I've heard all sorts of things about them. I wish I could read the Bible for myself, but where can a person get one?"

I wished that I could have helped her find a Bible, but I myself didn't know when I would again be able to hold the sacred Scriptures in my hands. Aunt Masha gave me a long worried look, then glanced at the door, hid her crucifix inside her clothing, and asked me, "Sasha, please don't betray me. You know yourself that if the KGB finds out about it, it will cause no end of trouble for me."

In winter the sun sets early, and so that Sabbath came to a close rather quickly. When I entered the dayroom I saw everybody talking in small groups. Some sat around tables, others situated themselves right on the floor.

In one group I spotted Tarzan. Noticing me, he waved to me to join them. "Sasha, come over here!" Obediently I followed his invitation and sat on the floor next to him. "Where did you disappear to?" Tarzan asked. "We thought you had already escaped while we worked." Everyone laughed, but Tarzan, without waiting for my answer, began to explain to me that "Saturday evenings here is our best time. Next day, being Sunday, everything is more relaxed around here. That's why we love to tell each other about our past escapades—who did what and how each got his money . . ."

He turned toward a boy that sat yoga style and said, "Hey, Cross-eyed, tell us how you robbed people. Explain to us your clever style. I have heard a lot about you from other thieves, and now we've finally met. Go right ahead and tell us all about it."

Everyone's attention focused on him. He was a puny fellow—about 15 with an upturned nose, thread-like narrow eyebrows, and equally thin lips. On his right cheek a large scar testified to his rowdy life. His tiny green eyes would occasionally draw inward, making him cross-eyed—hence his nickname. Generally, the felons there never called each other by their right name. They used such terms as Cross-eyed, Raven, Club, Hump, and others.

Cross-eyed scratched his head and, as if recalling something, began his story. "All right, perhaps I'll tell you how I used to clean out the pockets of train passengers. I had a chum named Vaska, whom we called Weasel. The two of us worked together. Ordinarily we did our thing during darkness. We waited for the right time when the train was approaching the platform, just when all the people were in a hurry to get aboard. The passengers were busy carrying baggage. Everyone knows that when people travel to distant places they usually have a lot of money on them. It was our perfect opportunity to check out their pockets.

"Weasel and I would mix into a crowd by the railroad cars, just like other passengers, and pretend we too were pushing to get inside. At the same time we searched everybody's pockets that we could. And if we did not find any money in that pocket and no one saw us, we would go through another. Until we became good at it, there were times when, because of our carelessness, someone would spot us and call for help. That's when we came to each other's aid.

"Let's say that a woman would yell that she was being robbed. I then, seeing that Weasel was in trouble, would run up to him and pull him away from the woman's grasp. And if someone tried to hold us, we always carried knives with us and brandished them. Man, by the time the cops would arrive, we would be long gone.

"In time we perfected our technique and learned how to cut open jacket and coat pockets with a sharp razor blade. I became so skillful that I could hold the razor blade between two fingers and lift the money with the other two.

"Sometimes one night's work could bring the two of us as much as 1,000 to 2,000 rubles. That's how much a worker earns in a whole year. Too bad that Weasel and I got caught when the cops set a trap for us. But that's all right. During the five years of my prison term I'll come up with better ideas—something new, more professional methods. This prison term for me will be the equivalent of a special 'degree' in the 'science of robbery.'"

When Cross-eyed finished, everyone sat staring at the floor, undoubtedly thinking about their own misdeeds. A dark-skinned boy with fine facial features and expressive brown eyes, who up to that time had not interacted with anyone, suddenly came to life. Rubbing his hands together, he began to talk in a rather lively voice, looking at all of his companions. "Well, 'eaglets,' how would you like to hear some heartrending stories from my murky past?"

"Go on, go on, Whitie," they all spoke at once, making themselves as comfortable as they could, ready to listen.

I didn't know why the dark-skinned fellow had such an ironic nickname. Apparently, according to the unwritten laws of prison life, such a name was not unusual, or maybe it implied some hidden meaning. Anyway, he smiled, took a heavy breath, and began. "Oh man, I wish I had a good smoke now to get me going. I would really be hot, and if we could add a shot of vodka on top of that, my tongue would really get loose, there would be no stopping me till morning . . ."

Unexpectedly he looked at me and said, "This little lamb, whose lips are still wet with his mother's milk, is sitting here among us and is probably thinking that he's in the company of devils. No, Sasha, we are not devils even though some people make us out to be. At one time we all were ordinary kids, just like any other young people, but life made us hard. Life first wrecks us, then we learn to adapt to it.

"Take me for example. I was born into a privileged, well-educated family. My mother is a director of a medical institute, and my father is a well-known journalist who writes many articles for newspapers and magazines. He even interviewed Khrushchev himself in the Kremlin several times. Both of my parents are dedicated Communists. We have everything at home, and I never lacked money to spend.

"I had a childhood dream—to become a famous painter. For several years I studied in the best school of fine arts. My teachers constantly told me that I had a great talent for painting. But although I loved doing nature scenes, more and more they made me draw various communist posters for holidays and parades. I despised all of that.

"As long as I compliantly fulfilled my assignments, everything went just fine, but as soon as I refused to portray what they wanted, my troubles began, both in the school of fine arts and at home with my parents. One day I decided to arrange a picture exhibition with a theme, the likes of which no one had ever seen. Locked in my room, I secretly painted pictures at night for almost a year. Perhaps they were distressing pictures, because I depicted gloomy night skies with dark clouds and cold autumn rain overflowing the banks of rivers and flooding homes where people slept. In one painting I depicted a cemetery with fresh graves, lit with weak moonlight. I even tried to draw pictures of the afterlife.

"Once I showed my work to one of my best friends. When he saw the pictures, he was so moved that he immediately offered to help me arrange an exhibition, beginning at our school and then shifting to some art gallery. On that same day we showed several of my pictures to the director of the school and to other teachers, but their reaction was totally negative. They said that my pictures were grotesque and not interesting, that at this point in time we had to show to the public the world of a happy society, the portrait of 'true communism.' They also said that it would have been good if I had tried to paint scenes showing people launching space ships to other planets, or children sending white doves into the sky.

"After numerous attempts to obtain a place for exhibit, we finally understood that no gallery would ever display such paintings. Then my friend suggested we arrange the exhibition right in his home. We chose 15 of my best canvasses, hung them on the walls of his house, and invited many of our friends from school and from our neighborhood. And so we had ourselves a small art festival.

"Our celebration did not last long. That same day someone called the police, and in the evening the authorities arrested me and confiscated all my paintings. They took me to police headquarters and summoned my parents. Also they called in the KGB representatives, who inspected all my work and without any discussion told my parents, 'If you want your life to remain trouble-free, you must destroy all this filthy trash with your own hands.

"They gave my father scissors, and he, bowing to the KGB threats, cut the canvases of all of my paintings right in front of my eyes, while two policemen held on to me just in case I wanted to make a fool of myself. At home my parents lambasted me for causing the family so much trouble. And to prevent similar incidents, my mother broke all my brushes.

"After a few days I ran away from home and began to live in the attics of large buildings. It was then that I fell into the company of thieves and became one myself in order to survive. During the daytime, while people were at work, we robbed apartments. At night I continued to paint my pictures, except this time not on canvas, but on the walls of buildings and railroad cars heading for Moscow. I invented a special paint mixture by adding creosol, used to treat railroad ties, and other chemicals that was virtually impossible to paint over.

"I began to paint protest slogans. 'Communism is a way to hell!' 'Away with Khrushchev, the boss of Communists, the chief liar!' 'We don't want to be slaves to Communism!' Also I depicted Lenin's face with horns. The railroad workers repeatedly tried to cover over my slogans, but when they realized that it wouldn't work, they hid my art with large red banners with communist slogans. The same thing presumably happened with the trains that traveled all the way to Moscow.

"I knew that sooner or later I would be caught. And I was. They brought me to the KGB headquarters, where they beat me so hard I did not regain consciousness for several days. After that they took me to court and gave me five years of imprisonment for anti-Soviet propaganda. Then they tried to make me admit that Communism was right in everything. They said if I would be obedient and comply with their wishes, life could be much better for me. I always despised them and will continue to hate them to my dying day.

"What kind of dim-witted fools must they be to display self-praising slogans on houses, bridges, streets, everywhere? For example: 'Glory to the great Soviet people, the builders of Communism!' To me it would seem just as stupid if in America they would hang posters that declared, 'Glory to the great American people, the builders of capitalism!' Or if I had written all over my own room, 'Glory to me, I'm the greatest!'

"And so, because I didn't care for any of it, my life had to change rather drastically, and I went downhill from there. My parents renounced me, rejecting their own son in order to continue their own way of life. Now I am all alone, but I don't think that I will perish.

"Of course, I could tell you a lot of other interesting things, but enough for now. Let someone else have a turn."

Tarzan, feeling himself the rightful leader of the group, poked another guy sitting next to him and said, "All right, Hump, it's your turn. Tell us your stuff."

Hump was a tall fellow with a broad, open face and massive arms totally covered with tattoos. He apparently wanted to begin his story, but at that moment the woman monitor, who had sat by the door all this time, got up from her seat, and everybody shut up. They did not want her to hear what they were talking about. She called one of the fellows and started asking him something. Tarzan nodded toward Hump and said, "All right, begin, we're listening."

"Mine was a different enterprise," he began. "We fleeced furniture stores. I figured that no other accumulated as much money as a large furniture store. Usually three or four of us 'worked' the store. Just before the store closed for lunch, we would enter it and select a good-sized cabinet, a closet, or a locker. Then we would ask a salesclerk for the keys under the pretext of wanting to inspect it. One of us would get inside the closet when no one was watching.

"Soon the salespeople would announce that they were closing the store for lunch. At that time we would go to the cashier and pay for that particular item with the agreement that as soon as they opened after lunch we would return with a truck to pick it up. After that everything went as smooth as butter. We would hire some truck driver and agree to pay him well if he would deliver the locker or whatever to a certain address.

"As soon as the store employees left the store for lunch, the fellow in the closet would climb out, open the safe with special tools, get all the money, and return to the piece of furniture. Then, after the lunch break, with the truck waiting in front, we would enter, show the receipt, carry out the object we had bought, load it on the truck, and ask the man to drive carefully to the indicated address while we sat in the back of the truck. On the way, at the right moment, we would jump off the truck. What followed after that was the best part. We would count the money, split it, and go on to another town to pull off another job."

Hump pulled out of his pocket a small piece of paper with some diagram drawings on it and began to explain something. But the bell rang, indicating it was time for the late night inspection. After the inspection, as we walked to our sleeping quarters, Tarzan stopped me and whispered into my ear. "Get a good night's rest. You'll need all the strength you can get. Tomorrow's your big 'E-Day.' I made all the arrangements for your escape and hope all goes well. I'll tell you more about it in the morning. Right now, go get some sleep."

CHAPTER 11

THE SECOND ESCAPE

SUNDAY MORNING I AWAKENED early while everybody else was still asleep. Not wanting to lose a moment, I decided to prepare for my breakout. After getting up quietly, I made my bed and slipped over to Tarzan's bed to go over everything with him. But he slept like a rock, apparently without a care in the world. At first I thought perhaps he had forgotten and was about to wake him up, but then after a few moments of hesitation, and not wanting to arouse suspicion, I returned to my bed and slid under the covers again.

The strangest thoughts about my escape kept creeping into my head. I imagined being lowered by rope through the window of the second story right onto the street. Or perhaps Tarzan and his friends knew of some secret passage through which they would lead me beyond the prison walls. But I had not the slightest idea what they really had in mind.

Thus I lay in bed until I heard the monitor order, "Everybody rise!" The quiet sleeping hall came to life. Everybody began to stir and make their beds while talking loudly among themselves. Somehow I had a feeling that I had very little time and had to be ready at any moment. After again quickly making my bed and completing my morning ritual, I stood by a window of our sleep-

197

ing hall and impatiently waited for further instructions.

Outside the window I saw the promise of a cheerful, sunny day. It was the beginning of February. Even though at night the temperature still fell below freezing, during the day winter was beginning its retreat, allowing the sun to shine brighter and a bit warmer. The bright sun now blinded my eyes, and the melting snow beyond the windows hinted at the inevitable end to the cold winter and the approaching spring.

A few minutes later Tarzan came up to me. In a particularly cheerful mood, he extended his hand to me in a friendly gesture and said, "Greetings to the honest at heart!" Then, sitting on the edge of my bed next to me, he began to talk quietly to me. "Listen to me very carefully! Today after breakfast is the best time for your breakout. My friends and I have an excellent plan for you. Try to remember everything I tell you.

"We have noticed that after breakfast a huge van-type truck leaves the yard of our prison at a specific time. What they carry we don't know, but that's not important. What's important is this. After breakfast I'll have my people posted around the whole prison in order to watch all the guards and other staff. They will strike up conversations with them, asking questions. In other words, they will distract anyone who might interfere with our plan. My boys know how to do that—I have no concern about them. It's you I'm worried about. I don't want you to carelessly ruin everything for yourself.

"When the time comes, I'll point out the truck to you. Then, as it moves toward our building, we will be watching it from the dining room window on the first floor. When it comes closest, you should quickly get outside and dash behind it so that no one can see you, since you'll be on the far side of the truck. The truck creeps toward the gate, and you should keep pace with the truck behind the rear wheel. You will be walking on the driver's side. If he should open the gate, he would definitely see you, but his companion always handles that task since he has the keys.

"Our prison is located on the corner of a narrow street. Therefore, as soon as the truck is out the gate, it will make a sharp turn to the right and stop to let the other man in after he locks the gate. At that very moment you should race into the alley to your left."

I drank in Tarzan's every word, trying to understand everything the first time. But I had an important question. "Tarzan, what happens if the dining room door is locked?"

He laughed slightly and patiently explained, "Before we thieves do any job, we check and double check every detail. Several times we have noticed that after breakfast, just before they lead us to the toilet, the door that leads outside is not locked. My boys will try to distract the guard at the door. They will keep him busy with questions or will point out something strange or important to him. But that's not your worry."

Everything that I had to do spun in my head. I wondered what someone might think if they saw me following the truck. A question popped into my head. "Won't the driver see me in his side-view mirror as I walk alongside the truck?"

Tarzan thought for a moment and then began to explain everything step-by-step. "Try to understand, Sasha. First of all, there is no traffic in the yard. Drivers generally approach the gate very slowly, and as the truck moves, they're busy double-checking their itinerary dockets and don't look around.

"Secondly, if you will keep close to his rear wheel, the chances of him spotting you in the mirror are extremely unlikely, because his mirror is adjusted to observe the passing lane. And in the third place, drivers usually glance at their sideview mirrors only on highways when they pass other vehicles or on turns. In the prison compound, where he has to drive mainly forward and only some 100 yards to the gate, he won't need the mirror at all. Trust me.

"But it's a good thing you're asking me about all these things. Obviously you're looking at it from all angles. But I'll have to tell you one more thing. No matter how carefully we work out the details, there is still always an element of risk. Same thing in this case—we did our best, but . . .

"Besides, I also think, if you really trust your God, and if He really exists, then you shouldn't have any doubts. He'll certainly help you, but you have to take risks. So don't sweat, it'll all turn out

OK." Then Tarzan gave me another serious look and asked, "Do you understand everything—what and how you should do it?"

I nodded decisively, but after some further thinking, asked, "If I have more questions, may I come to you before breakfast?"

Tarzan gave me a broad smile and in the same soft but firm voice answered, "You may, but only if nobody hears us. It would be better if we're not seen together." And after a short pause he added, "Of course there might be some unforeseeable complications, but it all depends on how well your luck goes."

We still had about an hour before breakfast, and I decided to be alone with my thoughts and pray. I was aware that by a sheer miracle a small opportunity was opening for me once again to gain my freedom, but that I needed to remain calm. Strangely, though, I didn't consider what would happen once I got out. It was still entirely possible that some old pastor or some other person could, offering his "valuable spiritual insight," again insist that it would be better for me to remain in prison in order to demonstrate my trust in God before the world. But I really did not think about it at that time. My whole being felt like a tightly wound-up spring. I was in a state of constant tension.

As I walked into the dayroom, I unexpectedly saw Anna Ivanovna. The encounter left me slightly dizzy. *Could this wicked woman be on duty today?* I thought. It meant that she would watch my every move, dooming our plan right from the start.

When she spotted me, she greeted me with a smile and said, "Sasha, you look fine. Others who have received a beating like yours can neither walk nor sit for weeks, but you're doing just fine. I think you're beginning to realize that no one is going to pet you around here. Even a children's prison has to have strict discipline. Order and discipline, as you well know, depend on unconditional obedience.

"We've been watching you now for several days and see that the rubber clubs helped you understand a number of things, and I am glad to find a change in your attitude. I can say we are all pleased that you have given up your foolish notions of escape from here. In fact, I am no longer worried about you.

"Tomorrow you'll get your head shaved, and you will look

just like the others. You will be given your prison garb, so you will fit right in." She spoke as though she was bearing good news, assuming that I would be somehow happy about it. "I expect that tomorrow, or at least by Tuesday, you'll be taken by train, along with many others, to your permanent destination."

The last words, "permanent destination," shook me up, and I asked, "What do you mean? Don't I have a set term that I have to serve right here in this prison? All of the others seem to have a specified amount of time to serve—some only three years, others five years for more serious crimes. But how about me?"

The instructor spread her arms and stuttered in confusion, "I don't really know how many years you need to serve in prison. The court didn't specify a term for you. Only one thing is clear: you have become a ward of the state, that's all. I don't know what else to tell you . . ."

In a hurt tone of voice I tried to protest. "So that means that I, like this battered table, have become the property of the government? And at someone's whim, as if they're moving this table from one room to another, I can be shipped from one place to another, and neither I nor my parents can know where they will ship me or for how long?"

Anna Ivanovna shrugged and in her usual cold voice said, "That doesn't concern me. There are other people whose job it is to decide what's to be done with you. Besides, I can't waste my time with you? This is my day off. I only stopped for a minute to pick up some papers I need to check over one last time. If you have any more questions, they can wait till tomorrow." Without another word she walked off.

A thought flashed in my head. *If she is gone for the day, that means the plan is still on and I should get ready.* I sat at one vacant table in a corner and began to go over all the details Tarzan had explained to me. Again and again I tried to picture in my mind how everything was to take place. "The most important thing is decisiveness, caution, and concentration," I kept reminding myself.

A number of things indicated that the day was a holiday, a Sunday. The first thing in the morning someone turned the television on, and anyone who cared could watch it. The monitor who generally sat by the door like a sentry now wandered casually in and out of the room. Anyone could do whatever he wanted, including playing games.

At last I heard the command to get ready for breakfast. It reminded me that I should prepare to escape. In the dining hall Tarzan sat beside me and kept repeating softly, "Be calm, Sasha. Don't gawk around. No one should suspect that you're about to do anything unusual."

He slid in front of me another bowl of rice and his cup of tea, broke off a lump of bread, and whispered, "Eat this portion too. You need all the strength you can get. Who knows when you will again be at a table."

I tried to push the bowl and the cup aside, but Tarzan again repeated, "I told you eat, so eat!"

We were first to finish our breakfast and left the table. I heard Tarzan whispering orders to "his boys" without looking at them. He called each one by his nickname. "Bobik, you go to the kitchen and start washing dishes and make sure none of the monitors get out until I tell you. Ask the women who work in the kitchen as many questions as you can think of, have an accident, break something. In other words keep everyone around you busy."

Bobik balked. "Hey, I never wash dishes; besides, that's not my—"

Tarzan cut him off. "You talk too much, Bobik. Just go and do what you're told now, then you can complain later." Next the gang leader called several other fellows and calmly issued orders, "Raven, you go upstairs and do your best to keep everyone from going downstairs. Did you hear what I told Bobik? Come up with all kinds of questions for the instructor or anyone else who gets in the way.

"Cross-eyed and Rat, you stand by the staircase and watch. If you notice any of the boys mess up things or if you see some of the prison staff coming down, alert me. I'll be standing at the bottom of the stairs by the door. And now, to your posts!"

Tarzan tried the door that led to the courtyard. As expected, it was not locked. Turning to me he said, "Slip through it without making a sound, and quickly get behind the truck. Once there, you are on your own. But just do as you were told. I hope you haven't forgotten my instructions."

Trying to stay calm, I replied that I remembered everything and that I would do my best to follow the plan.

Some in the dining hall were finished eating, others were taking their time, still poking at their food. Ordinarily during meals we could get up only to help ourselves to tea. But today, since it was Sunday, the monitor did not object even if someone left the dining area.

With everybody talking, it created a lot of noise and commotion in the room. Bent aluminum spoons clattered in the dented aluminum bowls. Everything seemed normal.

Tarzan and I stood by the window, and soon we saw the big truck being readied for its departure. "Well, Sasha," he said, "I hope in a few minutes you'll be beyond the barbed wire and out the gate. As we say here in prison to those who are released, 'Give our regards to freedom and don't forget those left behind!'"

Realizing that I really had only a few minutes left, I started rummaging through my pockets, hoping to find something I could leave with Tarzan as a memento, a fellow prisoner who, within only a few days, had become very close to me. But besides a clean piece of paper, a pencil, a plectrum, and a cherished ruble, I had nothing on me. Timidly I offered my ruble to him. "Thanks, pal, for everything. You did a lot for me, but unfortunately I don't have anything to thank you with for your help. Please take this ruble as a keepsake."

Laughing softly, he pushed my hand away. "I don't need any money here in prison. And if I do, I know where to get all I need. You don't know what awaits you beyond the gate. Your ruble might come in handy. Keep it. But, hey, if you really want to thank me, then say a prayer for me in your church. Maybe God will help me survive my five years in this rotten jail . . ." As he said it he angrily spat on the floor and rubbed it with his foot.

Nevertheless, I wanted to leave something for him. I got out my piece of paper and pencil and right on the windowsill quickly wrote a familiar Bible verse: "For God so loved the world, that

He gave His only begotten Son, that whosoever believeth in him should not perish, but have life everlasting."

After folding the piece of paper several times, I offered it to Tarzan. He smiled and, hiding it in his secret pocket, asked, "Is this another prayer for me?"

"No, this is a promise directly from God, who loves you and wants to save you," I answered.

Just then we saw the truck slowly start to move. A hint of excitement in his voice, Tarzan said, "That's it, Sasha. You're on!"

Again glancing around, we slipped out of the dining hall. One of Tarzan's guards gave us an "all clear" sign. I opened the door slightly, waiting for the rear end of the truck to pass alongside our building. Now if only no one would interfere during the next few moments.

My heart pounded so fast and so hard that I could feel it throughout my whole body. I felt like a wound up spring that at any moment could snap.

The truck inched closer and closer until its front wheels were almost even with the building. Its cab passed us, then the huge dark body of the truck that was about to shield me from sight. Finally the rear wheels came flush with our building. Here was my moment! Behind me I heard Tarzan's familiar voice. "Best of luck, Sasha!"

Like a bullet, I shot behind the truck. Overcoming my fear, I stayed close to the rear wheel and kept walking closer and closer to the entrance. As the truck slowly approached it, the driver's assistant jumped out, unlocked the padlock, and swung open the gate.

Through the narrow space between the truck and the gate I could already see the alley. Instantly I evaluated which direction held the best promise, left or right. Momentarily I felt the urge to just run for my life, but Tarzan's words echoed in my mind. *Take it easy or you'll ruin everything!* Edging closer to the wheel, I continued keeping pace with the vehicle.

Finally the truck cleared the gate of the prison compound and stopped for a few seconds while the assistant locked the gate. As the truck started to turn right and I saw that no one was nearby,

I jumped behind the truck, away from the side-view mirror, and took a sharp left. I sprinted toward the closest corner building, where I could hide behind it and get lost in the nearby alleys.

After covering some distance down one alley after another, I felt a bit safer and decided to catch my breath by slowing my pace somewhat. A quick glance around revealed no one watching me.

The sun continued to shine brightly and even warm the scene gently. The temperature was not quite as cold as during my previous escape. Now I had to decide where and to whom to run. I knew I could not place Konstantin in jeopardy a second time. If they had found me in his house last time, the authorities would have arrested him.

I remembered that our pastor lived in this part of town. Mother and I had visited his home several times, and I had an idea of how to get there. Knowing nobody else in the vicinity, I decided to run to his house—a distance of four or five miles.

By now I was beginning to feel the cold. Even though the sun shone, the temperature was still a few degrees below freezing. And I wore only what I had had on inside the prison. I had no hat and no coat. In spite of that, it seemed easier this time than the last. Could it be because of my prior experience?

To encourage myself, I kept saying the whole way, "Come on, come on, Sasha. Press on just a bit more! Don't get soft now! Keep running at least to the next building, and then you can walk." But after a few paces of walking, I began to push myself again. "Hurry up, hurry up! You don't have time! You have to make it before they discover your disappearance. And by the time they search your home or some other church members' homes, you should reach the safety of the pastor's house."

It never occurred to me that if they started searching the believers' homes, the pastor's house would be first on the list. My only thought at that time, however, was to keep my legs moving faster and cope with the shortness of breath. I don't know how long I ran, but I remember well that when I got to Pastor Demko's street, my body felt so cold that I could barely move.

And just as before, an unbearable fatigue and an uncontrollable desire to take a nap threatened to overwhelm me. I was exhausted.

If I could only sit for a while and rest a bit . . . But I remembered Konstantin's words: "Before people freeze to death, they feel fatigued and drowsy. And if they fall asleep just for a short time, that's the end of them." I felt as if the words scalded me, and I forced myself again to run, to walk, and then to run again.

Reaching the familiar gate, I knocked. The gate creaked, and I saw Aunt Katya, the pastor's wife. At first she shuddered from surprise when she saw me and then said, "Come in, come in. I bet you're freezing."

The pastor was not home. Rapidly I told the pastor's wife how I just had run away from the prison and asked her to hide me somewhere. After she heard my story, Aunt Katya said, "First of all, have something to eat, then rest later . . ." And she began to bustle around the kitchen.

A good-natured woman and a wonderful cook, she often whipped up a meal for unexpected guests. People came to her house at all times. And not just once. I too had partaken of the fine food of this hospitable home on a number of occasions.

Suddenly she turned around and in a frightened voice asked, "Sasha, you're not frostbitten are you?" After thoroughly checking my face, ears, cheeks, hands, and feet, she jubilantly exclaimed, "It's a miracle! Everything is normal, no signs of frostbite anywhere! Praise God! We'll warm you up inside with tea and honey, and you'll be just fine."

While I was still sitting at the table, Pastor Demko arrived home. I heard Aunt Katya joyfully announce to him in the hallway, "Misha, Misha, there is a surprise waiting for you in the kitchen! Sasha escaped again. He's here. It will be wonderful news for Nina."

As the pastor walked in, I noticed a happy smile on his face, and in his eyes tears of joy. He cried like a little boy and, wiping his tears with his hand, said, "Sasha, we prayed for you so very much. Even at night we prayed for you, and I never lost hope that God would perform some miracle. This is indeed a miracle!" Hugging me tightly, he kissed me on the back of my head.

But our rejoicing was short-lived. Uncle Misha, as I called him, suddenly became very serious and said softly, "We can't forget that the KGB won't rest when they find out that you've disappeared again. They will look for you everywhere. In one or two hours they may begin searching all the believers' houses. It is possible everything will turn out all right, but we cannot take any chances and must be prepared for anything.

"If we see someone suspicious approach our home, then you must quickly get out through this side door and hide in the shed." And he pointed to another door in the next room. The shed too had two doors. One led into the yard and the other into the side alley.

Pointing through a small window in the shed to a neighbor's house, he explained, "Sasha, should anything happen, you can run to the shed, from there into the street, and then across to that house. The people in that house are not believers, but they are kind sympathizers. And even though the man of the house has to be a party member, he hates the Communists. He has already helped our church members several times. I'll go there right now and alert him."

I went into the house, and in a few minutes Uncle Misha returned. He appeared calm and said to me, "Now, Sasha, you know some secrets about this house that only a very few people do. Perhaps some day it will come in handy. But for now you must catch up on your rest, because this very night you may have to begin a long journey."

When I opened my eyes I saw my Mother's smiling face. For a few moments I could not figure out where I was. I imagined I was still in prison, anticipating my impending escape. But when I rubbed my eyes, Mother was still there, and I heard her soft voice. "Oh, how happy I am to see you again, my precious one."

As I glanced around, I finally became totally awake. Our pastor, Konstantin, and three other members of our church entered the room. They looked at me with love and compassion, yet no one cried. Aunt Katya came in also and asked, "Are you hungry, Sasha? You have been sleeping for more than five hours now."

What do you mean five hours? I thought to myself. *I lay down for a nap just a few minutes ago.* But when I got up and stared out the window, I saw it was totally dark outside. After the tremendous and constant tension of my stay in prison and then the escape, for the first time I felt relaxed. The five hour "nap" I had had seemed like a few minutes.

While I had slept, the pastor had informed trusted church members of my escape, and they in turn had informed Mother and a few others that I was at the pastor's home. Now they were all here to discuss my fate.

We went into another room and sat around the table. The pastor rose and with a soft but triumphant voice announced, "We prayed hard for Sasha's deliverance from prison. What we have before us now is a miracle from God. After all that has happened, I cannot take the moral or spiritual responsibility upon myself to send this child back again into the devil's clutches— that prison from which he escaped for the second time. I don't believe he will get a third chance. It would be utterly foolish to permit such a thing. I am certain that God has helped us to make the right decision concerning Sasha. And now let's pray."

Almost everyone offered a short prayer for my safety and protection. After prayer, everybody went one by one to their homes, as it was already quite late. Only Mother and the pastor, with his wife, remained.

I was eager to know what plans they had made for me, so I asked the pastor, "Uncle Misha, why are we sitting around doing nothing? Any minute the police or the KGB could burst in, arrest everybody, and then what? We have to do something! I'm dying to know what you have decided to do with me."

The pastor heard me out patiently, then said nothing for a few moments. I realized that I had made a fool of myself, and was prepared to hear him repeat Tarzan's, "Cool it, or you'll ruin everything." But Uncle Misha smiled kindly and with the same calm voice said, "Everything is going according to plan, and you must learn to understand that we cannot speed up things beyond our control. But should the KGB or the police arrive, you already know what to do and where to run. So calm down and let's talk about the plan.

"You were already told to rest well because this night a long road awaits you. Just like all boys your age, I hope you too love train rides. Tonight you will leave on an extremely long journey to Siberia. Siberia has a large area called the Altay region. There among the ancient Altay Mountains, away from any big cities, you will have to spend some time in a small village.

"But Sasha, you must not forget that even in these remote Altay villages the KGB has its agents. It means that you will be expected to carefully follow the directions and advice of the people who will be taking care of you." He spoke to me as if he were reading to me some scary but interesting story, shifting between a whisper and a fairly loud volume.

When I heard that I had to go to Siberia, at first fear gripped me. I had read that Siberia was a frigid and inhospitable country that the government had used to exile political and criminal prisoners. But then it occurred to me that it would be easier to hide from the KGB in the Siberian region than here. I really did not care where they sent me as long as I was not in prison.

"Tonight you and another young woman from our church, Toma, will leave for Siberia. You know Toma, don't you?"

Suddenly I remembered the woman's name, even her face. When my former friend Mishka and I had started going to church, she would talk to us and then encouraged us to take part in singing church hymns.

When I answered that I knew her, the pastor continued, "Toma was recently discharged from work for religious reasons, so right now, while she is supposedly looking for a job, she will be accompanying you to your destination. She should be here any minute. It is vital, Sasha, for you to understand that you are about to enter an illegal status. This means that except for a very few trusted people, no one here should know where you're going—and where you came from. Once you reach your new home, you may even have to change your last name. At first it would be better for you to keep out of sight. You will spend most of your time in hiding. I know it won't be easy for you, but we see no other way out of this situation for the time being. What will happen later, only time will tell."

As I tried to picture what life in exile would be like, I felt as if I was going to another prison. But I had no other choice. At least I would spend my life during my "illegal status," as Uncle Misha termed it, among people of my faith who would never wish me ill. And this important fact comforted me.

Then the pastor turned to Mother. "I understand, Nina, that it's not easy for you, as a mother, to part with your son, for no one knows how long—maybe a year and maybe even longer. Everything will depend on circumstances. But please believe me, it is the best solution for Sasha."

"I understand everything," Mother said, wiping her tears, "and I am most thankful to you for your help and your love toward my son. Now I will feel better, knowing that Sasha will be among his own. I will miss him very much, but I will start saving money so I can visit him."

"You know, Nina," he interrupted, "I think that tomorrow or the following day you need to go to Sasha's prison. Pretend that you have remembered that he was to be sent away to another prison and that you have come to say goodbye to him. This way you will show that you have not heard of his escape. And then if they are looking for him, you can always use your visit as your excuse that you knew nothing about Sasha's escape and that you went to the prison to see him.

"They just might think that Sasha, after escaping, got lost somewhere or something else happened to him. And the fact that he escaped will be their responsibility, something they will have to answer for. It is possible that they, fearing investigation, will not request an all-out search for him, but will also pretend that everything is under control and that he is no longer there, but instead on the way to some other children's prison camp."

It was already late and Mother had to go home. Trying not to break into tears, she said as calmly as possible, "Here we are again, my son, having to say goodbye. . . . But I feel much better, because I am not leaving you in prison but in the care of kind people. Every day from early morning until late at night I will be thinking about you, because you, my son, are the most precious thing in the whole world to me. When you get a bit older, I will tell you all about my own difficult past and how you saved my life. . . ."

Grabbing her by her hand, I begged her to tell me now. But she brushed a tear from her face and answered, "Now is not the time, son. I need to go now, and I want to say a prayer before we part."

We knelt, and Mother offered a prayer that I will remember for the rest of my life. "Dear Lord, I thank You that You gave me this son! I am very grateful to You that after many trials I got to see him again! Today I dedicate him anew to You, Lord, and commit him into Your hands. Please save him for me! And give me strength to wait patiently for the day of our happy reunion, if not on this earth, then in eternity with You."

After the prayer Mother embraced me and kissed my eyes, my cheeks, my forehead, and even my nose. And I burst into tears. Mother wiped them away, saying, "Well, well, what is this, do I see a grown man crying? You did not cry in the prison, you really needn't cry here. Please get hold of yourself and be courageous."

Then she took from her purse her old Bible and, handing it to me, said, "I can't give you any special object for a keepsake, but what I am giving you is the most precious thing that I own. Oh, how much I want this Bible to help you become a good preacher." Then she reached into her purse again and pulled out a small blue notebook. "Use this little notebook like a diary to record the most significant events of your life."

In a sudden burst of excitement I hugged her. "Thank you! Thank you! For a long time I have wanted to have my own Bible, and now I do."

After we embraced one last time, she kissed me and left. Aunt Katya immediately set the table for tea and invited us to join her. "A good idea," Uncle Misha said. "While we wait for Toma we can chat a bit. I think, Sasha," he added, sipping his tea, "you will mature quite fast with all the trials and experiences that have come your way. My life was not very easy either. You know that by nationality I am German. And Germans were always under suspicion, especially during the war, and even now after the war.

"When I was young, I had to spend many years in a special prison camp just because I was German. I experienced a lot of hunger, cold, and many other hardships, and not only I, but tens of thousands of other Germans like me. But that is another matter that could fill volumes of sad stories.

211

"Later my whole family and I moved to Ust-Kamenogorsk, where I encountered Adventists. I was baptized, married, and began my Christian life, my walk with the Lord. At first there was only a small group of us, but as the number of church members increased, we decided to find us a building for our worship services. From that day on we began to have troubles with the KGB. They arrested me several times and kept me in solitary confinement for days at a time. But so far God has protected me, and I am amazed that by some miracle I'm still free. Many, many pastors are languishing in prisons.

"I am certain that soon they will arrest me too. As one chekist told me once, 'The prison is crying for you, Demko.' It is the kind of times we are living in now, and there is no way out. I am ready to go to prison even right now, except that I feel sorry for my wife. As you know we have no children.

"The biggest problem for the church is that many of its members, deacons, and even pastors have been intimidated into selling themselves to the KGB and now are working with them. Maybe you have heard about one member of our church in Dubovoy? He reported to the KGB absolutely everything: where the secret meetings were being held, who preached, who distributed the Sabbath school lessons and other printed material.

"When we were thoroughly convinced that he was the informer, we stopped including him in our underground activities. Now he receives no religious literature, so he has nothing to relay to the KGB. There are other unidentified traitors among us, but we cannot suspect everybody. So at any time we expect just about anything to happen.

"Just recently someone told me about an incident that occurred in one of our neighboring Adventist churches. There a young man named Boris was baptized. His model Christian behavior fooled all the church members. One time when Boris was attending an underground service in a home occupied by some old members of the church, their son, who was not a believer himself and who just happened to be there, recognized Boris. This son of Adventist parents worked as a chauffeur for the KGB and had seen Boris at headquarters every day and knew him to be a KGB officer.

"No one had even imagined such a possibility. Moreover, the church leaders had grand plans for him. They were preparing Boris for ordination for pastoral duties, yet he turned out to be a most dedicated persecutor of the church. When everything came out into the open, the church disfellowshiped him. He in turn had the pastor locked up in a high security prison for five years. I could cite many similar incidents.

"The chekists have attempted to recruit me several times too. I remember one time they caught me at a secret church service, arrested me, and brought me to the KGB station, where some official wanted to talk with me. He asked me, 'What kind of salary do you get for your work, Michael?'

"I told him that my income was 120 rubles a month. He said, 'If you will work for us, I can promise you twice that amount.'

"I thought for a while, then told him, 'You want to buy me cheaply, comrade officer. When Christ lived on our earth, Satan promised Him the whole world just for one bow. Even then Christ refused. And you want me to sell out my Lord for 240 rubles?'

"I remember they gave me quite a trashing for that. They told me afterward, 'When you go home, say goodbye to your family, because very soon you will suddenly disappear for good. We know how to do these things, and you may consider this to be our promise to you.'

"So I have been living in constant expectation ever since. So far, the Lord has been good to me. He has protected me from day to day, though what will happen in the future remains to be seen."

I was so engrossed in his narrative that I completely forgot about my tea and sat spellbound listening to him.

"Now is that time, Sasha, when the faithful and the unfaithful church members, the true pastors and those that can be bought, are being tested," he continued. "Difficulties and trials for a Christian are like the hardening of metal. In order to temper the metal, it has to be heated until it is red hot and then submerged into cold water. This is how our heavenly Father is trying His children. It is good if we remain faithful, but if not . . ."

Suddenly someone knocked three times on the window. Aunt Katya got up and said, "I will open the door, it's Toma."

"How do you know it's Toma?" I asked.

"How many knocks did you hear?" Uncle Misha inquired.

"I think there were three," I answered.

"You're right. When we hear three knocks, we know it is one of our people. That is our agreement."

Toma walked into the kitchen where we were sitting. A woman of about 25, she was a quite tall, pleasant person. Mild frost made her cheeks pink and her hair, peeking from under her knitted cap, slightly white. Her brown eyes looked at me cheerfully from under her dark eyelashes as she stood in the doorway. "Are you ready for some serious travel, Sasha?" she asked. "I have already bought the tickets, and we will leave in a few minutes." She opened a large bag and suggested, "If you have anything to take with you, you can put it here."

We packed the things my mother had brought for me from home and were all dressed and ready to go. Uncle Misha once more looked at the time and said, "Now it is half past midnight. I made some arrangements with one of our neighbors with a car to take you to the train station. I will walk you there."

In the doorway Uncle Misha hugged me again, then looking straight at me, said, "In your new home, Sasha, think about your mother's wish for you to become a good preacher. Soon we will need pastoral replacements, and you already have had an experience with God. Besides, you are endowed with many talents. So here is my advice: since a whole year will pass before you will be able to return to school, you can use this time to start preparing yourself for God's service. Think about it! And may God bless you!"

I felt he wanted to tell me more, but there was no time. After a short parting prayer we began our journey.

The train station, as usual, was crowded. Cigarette smoke mixed with the odor of sweat-permeated clothes filled the large waiting room. People often had to wait for days for their connecting trains. The general noise and the hum of many voices, mingled with children's cries, reverberated from the top of the enormously high ceiling. All the benches were occupied, and many people sat on the floor, on stair steps leading to the second story, and even on window sills. After the peaceful atmosphere in the pastor's home, the noise in the station sounded like chaos.

We entered the waiting room and stopped near the door. Toma asked me to guard our things for a few minutes while she checked on the track, platform, and time of departure of our train.

When she left, I began to watch the people around me. It felt wonderful to realize that I had nothing at the moment to fear. I just stood there and stared at everything.

Not far from me a group of five peasants situated themselves on the floor and began to play cards on a suitcase in the center. On the other side of the walkway several hefty policemen dragged two unconscious drunks from between the benches toward the exit. A young woman changed her infant's diapers on her lap while two Gypsy kids approached everybody, crying and begging for a few kopeks to buy bread.

Suddenly among the multitude of faces I saw a familiar woman. At first I could not place her though I noticed that she was also staring intently at me. When I saw her moving toward me, I suddenly remembered that she was one of the monitors at the Youth Allocation Center, and worse yet, that she recognized me.

In an instant all the station noise seemed to cease. I felt dead silence all around. All I saw now was the approaching woman and nothing else. Towering over me, she demanded, "What are you doing here, Sasha? Who are you with? I am meeting some friends of mine, but why are you here? Don't you know where you belong?"

Instantly realizing that I was dressed in someone else's clothes, transforming my appearance somewhat, I calmly answered, "I am sorry, you have mistaken me for someone else. I am not Sasha. My name is Vitya Zhukov."

The monitor took another look at me, and without saying a word, turned and quickly went through the hall toward the door over which hung a large sign: "Station Police." Not needing anyone to tell me what would happen next, I knew I had to act immediately.

Grabbing the bags, I shot outside like a bullet. After the bright lights inside the hall, I could not see a thing outside. I just dashed straight ahead. After a few seconds I gradually began to make out the outlines of large buildings and trees around me. Soon I could clearly see where I was. I had just crossed the square in front of the railroad station, and now I was on the side of a small park. Running a bit further, I hid behind some trees and watched the entrance to the railroad station.

In a few minutes I saw Toma race out of the station in another direction, then suddenly turn and head toward the trees where I was hiding. I waited until she came closer, and then I called to her softly. "Toma, I'm here. Come here. Let me tell you what happened . . ."

The woman located the direction of my voice. Then I slipped out from behind the trees and waved at her. No sooner was she out of plain view and behind the trees than a police car with several police officers pulled up to the station entrance. From the cover of darkness and the trees we continued to observe the train station.

The police quickly surrounded the station. Some of them simply ran back and forth on the platform, checking out various buildings of the terminal complex. It was obvious that staying even under the cover of the trees where Toma and I were was becoming more risky by the minute.

"Don't you think we had better get out of here?" she whispered. "Any minute the police may start combing this wooded area."

My whole body shook from fear, and I felt that running away now was useless. The police would find me anyway. What was the use of trying to escape. Evidently Toma sensed my panic and began to talk to me in a calm voice. "Sasha, you should understand that remaining here near the station makes no sense. Trying to leave on the train is also impossible, because the police will stand at each entrance and will check every passenger. The only thing left for us to do is to hide at some trustworthy person's home for a few hours, and in the morning catch a bus to any small town where the train stops. There we could board and be on the way to Novosibirsk."

"What about our tickets?"

"Don't worry about them. The most important thing is to get away from the police. I have enough money for new tickets. For now we have no other alternative."

Both of us grabbed our bags and ran through the trees toward the park exit, away from the terminal. Finally we ended up on an unfamiliar empty street. At the intersection we read the street sign, trying to orientate ourselves. We kept walking and reading street signs until we found a familiar street.

"You know what, Sasha," Toma said, stopping me, "I have an aunt living close by all by herself. Even though she is not a Christian, she is a kind woman. Maybe she will let us stay with her for a few hours, and from there we can easily find our way to the bus station."

Toma's aunt, Luba, was indeed a kind woman. Despite the fact that it was dead of night, she opened the door and let us in. Quickly Toma explained what had happened and asked her to allow us stay there for at least a couple hours. I was so exhausted that it seemed I fell asleep before my head hit the pillow. Then the next moment someone was shaking me. Unable to open my eyes, I jumped up in fear and confusion, asking in a bewildered voice, "What's wrong? What's going on?"

Hugging me tightly, Toma whispered into my ear, "Sasha, dear, calm down! You have already slept for three hours, and it is time for us to leave."

In a few more minutes I was completely awake, and ignoring a bad headache and a slight nausea from such a nightmarish night, we left the house. It was still totally dark. Not a person or car stirred on the street. As we walked, Toma laid out her plan for the day. She and her aunt had hardly slept at all as they discussed the best way to leave the city unnoticed. Aunt Luba had an excellent idea. Instead of going to the bus station, she suggested we get on the bus at the stop near her house. She took that same bus whenever she went to visit relatives in a neighboring town. Also she knew of a railroad station in the neighboring town, from which we could catch a train to Novosibirsk. Furthermore, what was most important for us, the train would bypass our city of Ust-Kamenogorsk. After Toma had explained everything to me, I felt so full of energy that I was ready not only to walk, but to run toward the bus stop.

When we reached the bus stop, it was still dark, and only a weak glow appeared on the eastern horizon, announcing the dawn of a new day. Frost shimmered in the air, but we were dressed warmly and did not feel the cold. All our attention now totally focused on getting on that bus. In about 15 minutes it arrived, and I happily found a window seat. Soon the silhouettes of houses and buildings drifted past. I watched as the streets of my town faded into the distance.

The four-and-a-half hour ride provided me with much needed sleep. When I awoke, the bus had reached its destination, and it was time to get off. Luckily we did not have to wait long at the railroad station. But even during those couple hours I constantly imagined that the police and everyone else were watching me with suspicion. Nervous and jumpy, I was ready to flee instantly.

Finally even those fears were behind me. Our train arrived on time, and once inside the compartment we were finally able to breathe a sigh of relief, knowing that we were reasonably safe and that now no one was about to snatch me and drag me back to prison. There was no one else in our compartment as yet. It was pleasant to sit by the window, listen to the rhythmic knocking of the wheels, and watch the changing countryside.

Toma said that she was extremely tired and was going to bed down. By now I was wide awake and continued to sit by the window watching the world go by, relishing the feeling of safety and security. It was quiet in the compartment, and my thoughts drifted. I don't know why, but I kept reflecting on life's unfairness, how I had seemingly been dealt an disproportionately large share of troubles. *Why is it that my brother and sister live without any care and don't have to worry about tomorrow,* I kept wondering. *I, in contrast, as though cursed, have to constantly be on the run and live in fear. Even Mother's lot is by far easier than mine. Yes, the authorities took her to court and deprived her of her maternal rights. However, she is still at home. But I had to suffer in prison, and now here I am, going I know not where. Life for her should be better now. Nobody will be ar-*

resting her because of me, and she can live peacefully among her friends and her familiar surroundings. She can sleep in her own bed, but I will have to constantly face the unknown.

Then I suddenly remembered Mother's words: "When you grow up a bit, Sasha, I will tell you how you saved my life." Instantly I realized that she had also had a difficult life. I could not recall her ever taking any days off from work, much less having a vacation. Nor had I ever seen her husband giving her any moral support. He never helped her in anything or bought her any presents. My stepbrother and stepsister were really not her children, but sometimes I felt that she gave them more care and affection than she even did me, which often brought me to tears.

Even though it was only in part, I think I at last began to understand that my mother had suffered tremendously when her own child had been torn from her and became a ward of the court. Now, though not in a prison camp, I still would be in the care of strangers. Of course she could not have been worry-free or happy about it. Her thoughts were constantly of me. And now I felt ashamed for allowing myself to compare myself to her, to think even for a moment that her life was easier than mine.

It was already getting dark outside when I decided to lie down in my compartment berth. Staring at the ceiling, I continued to wonder what the future had in store for me. Without my realizing it, the wings of memory carried me back to my early childhood. One after another the scenes of my life floated before me. I watched myself as a mischievous boy pulling pranks on my neighborhood friends. I saw the beginning of school . . . my first, yet ardent love of Larissa . . . times of inseparable friendship with Mishka . . . my initial experience at a church service and my first interest in religion . . . then my decision to become a Christian, followed by the problems that resulted from it . . . my friend Mishka abandoning me . . . all my neighborhood friends hating me . . .

Mockery at school . . . the car accident that I miraculously survived . . . the confrontations with the chekists during my early days in church and at home . . . the terrible time when we were evicted from our apartment and had to live in the shed . . . the court trial and its verdict . . . prison . . . escape . . . again prison and being

beaten half to death . . . another escape . . . the previous night's encounter with the woman monitor from the prison compound—
truly I had been was only minutes from being apprehended.
Another flight and hide-out just to survive. And all of these nightmarish experiences just to be facing yet still more unknown.

These depressing thoughts weighed heavily on my heart. The
loneliness and feelings of melancholy made me want to cry.
Getting up again, I sat by the window. Outside, moonlight
spread over the even snow. Lights from the houses kept vanish-
ing in the night as the train took me closer and closer to the mysterious Siberian wasteland.

In my fantasy I imagined living in a tiny hut among the dense
forests of the Altay mountains. Maybe during the night wild animals would peep in its windows. Perhaps it would be scary for
me there, unbearable, lonely . . .

"And then it may not be like that at all," I said to myself.
"Maybe it will be the best time of my life, when I can think about
Mother's and Uncle Misha's wishes for me and begin my preparation and training for ministerial service. Who knows what lies
ahead? What might my future be?"

Just then I remembered the little blue notebook mother had
given me as we said goodbye. I felt a burning desire to make my
first entry in it. After all, I was about to take my first step into a
new phase of my life. Taking the cherished little book, I started
to record some of the previous events of my life. But before I did,
I paused, then decided that perhaps it might be more interesting
if I began with whatever waited ahead of me.

Therefore on the very first page of the diary in bold letters I
wrote: "Today, 23rd of February, Monday, 1964. I begin my life
in self-exile, a life on the run. What sort of life it will be, I have
no clue." At the end of the entry I placed a huge question mark.

My eyelids grew heavy, and I had a hard time keeping them
open as the even swaying of the passenger car lulled me to
sleep. The rhythmic knocking of the wheels incessantly repeated my question in my head: "What is ahead? What is
ahead? What is ahead?"

EPILOGUE

DURING FEBRUARY 1964 I secretly arrived at the small and remote Siberian town of Gorno-Altaisk. The tall mountains surrounding it made me feel cut off from the rest of the world. For a whole year I lived in an illegal limbo. Except for my mother and the pastor of my church, no one knew where I was.

A single Adventist woman took me in. During that entire time I could not go outside except when it was dark, and even then only for brief periods. Such total isolation naturally frustrated an active boy of 12.

The small house I lived in had no electricity. I read much religious material by the light of a kerosene lamp and even copied several books by hand. They included Ellen White's *Steps to Christ* and *The Great Controversy*. Those lonely days were my preparation for pastoral service.

A year later my parents moved from the Kazakh Republic to the large Siberian city of Barnaul, and I was finally permitted to go home to them. Of course when I began to attend school I again confronted many problems because of Sabbath observance. Baptized at 15, I became totally absorbed in church service. At first I became a leader of the children's group and later the youth department.

The Seventh-day Adventist denomination appointed me as a church worker at the age of 16 for several small groups. Every Sabbath I preached and prepared people for baptism. God blessed my efforts, and the groups grew rapidly. But such success disturbed the government and brought on new persecution. One night the authorities arrested our pastor and his wife, and the next day the KGB came after me. I escaped only because I was not at home when they arrived. However, it was obvious that I could not remain in that city, and once again I had to flee, this time to another Siberian city, Novokunzetsk. There I spent two years working as the assistant to the local pastor.

The government drafted me into the army when I was 19. I spent the next two years coping with the many problems that military service created for a believer. Shortly before my discharge my mother died, and from that day on I felt like an orphan.

When I was 21, the local Adventist conference called me to be a pastor, although I did not begin pastoral service until a month after I married Vera Khiminets at the age of 22. I served as pastor of both large and small churches throughout the Soviet Union. One of the churches had more than 1,000 members. Other times I worked in small communities that did not have a single Adventist. Usually I had to work underground because of the strict laws against religious proselytizing. Besides pastoral duties, I also served as a secretary-treasurer in one of the largest conferences at that time. During the almost 20 years I spent working for the church, I experienced many incredible miracles as God protected me from the KGB. But those stories are for another time.

Vera and I had two children, a son, Vladislav, and a daughter, Ella. Because of the rough life I had lived, I determined to provide a better future for them, especially in the area of a Christian education. About this time the situation in my country began to improve as it offered its people more freedom. Our family received an invitation from Adventist friends in the United States to come to California.

With the help of our new American friends, our children had the opportunity to attend an Adventist school. After completing the course at Fresno Adventist Academy, Vladislav enrolled at Pacific Union College, where he studied for two years. My daughter, Ella, also graduated from the same academy and now studies in a local city college, but hopes to complete her studies at an Adventist school.

At the same time I have been able to study theology at a local seminary and earn a Master of Divinity degree. I have also been doing volunteer preaching in a California Adventist church. My wife has worked hard to help support us while we studied. Some day I hope to return to my homeland and pastor there.